Jacob Boehme

SELECTIONS

OF TRUE REPENTANCE

☙

OF TRUE RESIGNATION

☙

THE SUPER SENSUAL LIFE

☙

OF HEAVEN AND HELL

☙

THE WAY FROM DARKNESS
TO TRUE ILLUMINATION

Of True Repentance

by Jacob Boehme 1575-1624,
The Teutonic Theosopher

SHOWING
HOW MAN SHOULD STIR HIMSELF UP
IN
MIND AND WILL
AND
WHAT HIS EARNEST CONSIDERATION AND
PURPOSE SHOULD BE

How Man must stir himself in Mind and Will; and what his Consideration and earnest Purpose must be, when he will perform powerful and effectual Repentance: And with what Mind he must appear before God, when he would ask, so as to obtain, Remission of his Sins.

Brought forth in the 1600's by a humble shoemaker; translated into English over 100 years later; suppressed and hidden away until recently in theological archives around the world... a worthy personal study not just for academics but for all those who are spiritually grounded in the WORD, who are learning to hear the Lord, and who hunger for more.

THE SIGNATURE OF ALL THINGS. A drawing from the 1730 edition of the Works of Jacob Boehme showing definite Rosicrucian influences.

Jesus said unto Nicodemus, Verily, verily I say unto thee, Except a Man be born again, he cannot see the Kingdom of God. Nicodemus saith unto Him, How can a Man be born when he is old? Can he enter the second Time into his Mother's Womb and be born? Jesus answered, Verily, verily, I say unto thee, Except a Man be born of Water, and of the Spirit, he cannot enter into the Kingdom of God. That which is born of the Flesh is Flesh, and that which is born of the Spirit is Spirit. Marvel not that I said unto thee, Ye must be born again. The Wind bloweth where it listeth and thou hearest the Sound thereof, but canst not tell whence it cometh, and whither it goeth: So is every one that is born of the Spirit.

John 3, 3-8

What is a Man profited if he should gain the whole World, and lose his own Soul? or What shall a Man give in exchange for his Soul?

Matt. 16, 26

THE AUTHOR'S PREFACE TO THE READER.

Dear Reader,

If thou wilt use these Words aright, and art in good Earnest, thou shalt certainly find the Benefit thereof. But I desire thou mayest be warned, if thou art not in Earnest, not to meddle with the dear Names of God, in and by which the most High Holiness is invoked, moved, and powerfully desired, lest they kindle the Anger of God in thy Soul. For we must not abuse the Holy Names of God. This little Book is only for those that would fain repent, and are in a Desire to begin. Such will find what Manner of Words therein, and whence they are born. Be you herewith commended to the Eternal Goodness and Mercy of God.

OF
TRUE REPENTENCE

When Man will enter upon Repentance, and with his Prayers turn to God, he should, before he beginneth to pray, seriously consider the State of his own Soul. How it is wholly and altogether turned away from God, become faithless to Him, and only bent upon this temporary, frail, and earthly Life; bearing no sincere Love towards God and its Neighbor, but wholly lusting and walking contrary to the Commandments of God, and seeking itself only, in the temporal and transitory Lusts of the Flesh.

2. In the next Place, he should consider that all this is an utter Enmity against God, which Satan hath raised and wrought in him, by his Deceit in our first Parents; for which Abomination's Sake we must suffer Death, and undergo Corruption with our Bodies.

3. He should consider the three horrible Chains wherewith our Souls are fast bound during the Time of this earthly Life. — The First is the severe Anger of God, the Abyss, and dark World, which is the Center, Root, or constituent Principle of the Soul's Life. The Second is the Desire of the Devil against the Soul, whereby he continually sifteth and tempteth it, and without Intermission striveth to throw it from the Truth of God into his own evil Nature and Element, viz. into Pride, Covetousness, Envy, and Anger; and with his Desire, bloweth up and kindleth those evil Properties in the Soul, whereby its Will turneth away from God, and entereth into SELF. The Third and most hurtful Chain of all, wherewith the poor Soul is tied, is the corrupt and altogether vain, earthly, and mortal Flesh and Blood, full of evil Desires and Inclinations. Here he must consider that he lies close Prisoner with Soul and Body in the Mire of Sins, in the Anger of God, in the Jaws of Hell; that the Anger of God burneth in him in Soul and Body, and that he is that very loathsome Keeper of Swine, who hath spent and consumed his Father's Inheritance, namely, the precious Love and Mercy of God, with the fatted Swine of the Devil in earthly Pleasures, and hath not kept the

dear Covenant and Atonement of the innocent Death and Passion of Jesus Christ; which Covenant God of mere Grace hath given or put into our Humanity, and reconciled us in Him. He must also consider that he hath totally forgotten the Covenant of Holy Baptism, in which he had promised to be faithful and true to his Saviour, and so wholly defiled and obscured his Righteousness with Sin, (which Righteousness, God had freely bestowed upon him in Christ), that he now stands before the Face of God, with the fair Garment of Christ's Innocency which he hath defiled, as a dirty, ragged, and patched Keeper of Swine, that hath continually eaten the Husks of Vanity with the Devil's Swine, and is not worthy to be called a Son of the Father, and Member of Christ.

4. He should earnestly consider that wrathful Death awaiteth him every Hour and Moment, and will lay hold on him in his Sins, in his Garment of a Swine-Herd, and throw him into the Pit of Hell as a forsworn Person and Breaker of Faith, who ought to be reserved in the dark Dungeon of Death to the Judgement of God.

5. He should consider the earnest and severe Day of God's Final Judgement, when he shall be presented living with his Abominations before God's Tribunal. That all those whom he hath here offended or injured by Words and Works, and caused to do Evil, (so that by his Instigation or Compulsion they also have committed Evil), shall come in against him, cursing him before the Eyes of Christ and of all Holy Angels and Men. That there he shall stand in great Shame and Ignominy, and also in great Terror and Desperation, and that it shall forever grieve him to reflect that he hath fooled away so glorious and eternal a State of Salvation and Happiness, for the Pleasure of so short a Time; and that he had not taken care in that short Time to secure to himself a Share in the Communion of the Saints, and so to have enjoyed with them Eternal Light, and Divine Glory.

6. He must consider that the ungodly Man has lost his Noble Image - God having created him in and for His Image or creaturely Representation - and has gotten instead thereof a deformed or monstrous Shape, like a hellish Worm or ugly Beast.

Wherein he is an enemy to God, to Heaven, and to all Holy Angels and Men, and that his Communion is, and will be forever, with the Devils and hellish Worms in horrible Darkness.

7. He must earnestly consider the eternal Punishment and Torture of the Damned; how that in eternal Horror they shall suffer Torments in their Abominations which they had committed here, and may never see the Land of the Saints to all Eternity, nor get any Ease or Refreshment, as appears by the Example of the Beggar and the rich Man.

All this a Man must earnestly and seriously consider, and remember also that God had originally created him in such a fair and glorious Image, even in His own Likeness, in which He, Himself, would dwell. That He created him out of His Goodness, for Man's own eternal Bliss and Glory, to the End that he might dwell with the Holy Angels and Children of God in great Happiness, Power, and Glory; in the Eternal Light; in the praiseful and melodious Harmony of the Angelical and Divine Kingdom of Joy. Where he should rejoice continually with the Children of God, without Fear of any End. Where no evil Thoughts could touch him, neither Care nor Trouble, neither Heat nor Cold. Where no Night is known; where there is no Day or limited Time any more, but an everlasting Blessedness, wherein Soul and Body tremble for Joy. And where he, himself, should rejoice at the infinite Wonders and Virtues appearing in the Brightness of Colors, and the Variety of Splendor opened and displayed by the Omnipotent Powers and Glories of God, upon the new crystalline Earth, which shall be as Transparent Glass. And that he doth so willfully lose all this Eternal Glory and Happiness for the Sake of so short and poor a Time, which even in this State of Vanity and Corruption, in the evil Life of the voluptuous Flesh, is full of Misery, Fear, and utter Vexation; and wherein it goeth with the Wicked as with the Righteous, as the one must die, so must the other; only the Death of the Saints is an Entrance into the Eternal Rest, while the Death of the Wicked is an Introduction into the eternal Anguish.

8. He must consider the Course of this World, that all Things in it are but a Play, wherewith he spends his Time in such Unquietness; and that it goes with the Rich and Mighty as with the Poor and the Beggar. That all of us equally live and move in the four Elements; and that the hard-earned Morsel of the Poor is as relishing and savoury to him in his Labour, as the Dainties of the Rich are to him in his Cares. Also, that all of us subsist by one Breath, and that the rich Man hath nothing but the Pleasures of the Palate and the Lust of the Eye, for a little while more than his poor Neighbor, for the End of both is the Same. Yet for this short-lived Lust's Sake, many foolishly forego so inconceivable a Happiness, and bring themselves into such extreme and eternal Misery.

In the deep Consideration of these weighty Truths, Man shall come to feel in his Heart and Mind, especially if he at the same Time represents and sets before his own Eyes his own End, a hearty Sighing and Longing after the Mercy of God, and will begin to bewail his committed Sins; and to be sorry he has spent his Days so ill, and not observed or considered that he stands in this World as in a Field, in the growing to be a Fruit either in the Love or in the Anger of God. He will then first begin to find in himself that he has not yet labored at all in the Vineyard of Christ, but that he is a dry fruitless Branch of the Vine.

And thus in many a one, whom the Spirit of Christ touches in such a Consideration, there arises abundant Sorrow, Grief of Heart, and inward Lamentation over the Days of his Wickedness which he hath spent in Vanity, without any Working in the Vineyard of Christ.

Such a Man, whom the Spirit of Christ thus brings into Sorrow and Repentance, so that his Heart is opened both to know and bewail his Sins, is very easily to be helped. He needs but to draw to himself the Promise of Christ, viz. That God willeth not the Death of a Sinner but that He wisheth them all to come unto Him, and He will refresh them; and, that there is great joy in Heaven for one Sinner that repenteth. Let such a one but lay hold on the Words of Christ and wrap himself up into His meritorious Passion and Death.

But I will now speak to those who feel indeed in themselves a Desire to repent, and yet cannot come to acknowledge and bewail their committed Sins. The Flesh saying continually to the Soul, Stay a while, it is well enough; or it is Time enough tomorrow; and when tomorrow is come, then the Flesh says again, Tomorrow; the Soul in the meanwhile, fighting and fainting, conceiveth neither any true Sorrow for the Sins it hath committed nor any Comfort. Unto such a one, I say, I will write a Process or WAY, which I myself have gone, that he may know what he must do, and how it went with me, if peradventure he be inclined to enter into and pursue the same; and then he will come to understand what he shall find here afterwards written.

The Process of Repentance; or WAY to Conversion

When any Man findeth in himself by the former or any other Considerations, pressed Home upon his Mind and Conscience, a Hunger or Desire to repent, and yet feeleth no true Sorrow in himself for his Sins which he hath committed, but only a Hunger or Desire of such Sorrow, so that the poor captive Soul continually sighs, fears, and must needs acknowledge itself guilty of Sins before the Judgement of God. Such a one, I say, can take no better Course than this, namely, to wrap up his Senses, Mind, and Reason together, and make to himself instantly, as soon as ever he perceiveth in himself the Desire to repent, a mighty strong Purpose and Resolution that he will that very Hour, nay, that very Minute, immediately enter into Repentance, and go forth from his wicked Way, and not at all regard the Power and Respect of the World. Yea, and if it should be required, would forsake and disesteem all Things for true Repentance Sake; and never depart from that Resolution again, though he should be made the Fool and Scorn of all the World for it.

But that with the full Bent and Strength of his Mind, he will go forth from the Beauty and Pleasure of the World, and patiently enter into the Passion and Death of Christ in and under the Cross, and set all his Hope and Confidence upon the Life to come. That even now in Righteousness and Truth he will enter into the Vineyard of Christ, and do the Will of God. That in the Spirit and Will of Christ he will begin and finish all his Actions in this World, and for the Sake of Christ's Word and Promise, which holds forth to us a Heavenly Reward, willingly take up and bear every Adversity and Cross so that he may be but admitted into the Communion or Fellowship of the Children of Christ and in the Blood of the Lamb, Jesus Christ, be incorporated and united unto His Humanity.

He must firmly imagine to himself, and wholly wrap up his Soul in this Persuasion, that in his Purpose he shall obtain the Love of God in Christ Jesus, and that God will give unto him according to His faithful promise, that Noble Pledge, the Holy Ghost, for an Earnest; that, in the Humanity of Christ, as to the Heavenly Substance, he shall be born again in himself, and that the Spirit of Christ will renew his Mind with His Love and Power, and strengthen his weak Faith. Also that in his Divine Hunger he shall get the Flesh and Blood of Christ for Food and Drink, in the Desire of his Soul, which hungereth and thirsteth after It as its proper Nutriment; and with the Thirst of the Soul drink the Water of Eternal Life out of the Sweet Fountain of Jesus Christ, as Christ's most true and steadfast Promise is.

He must also wholly and firmly imagine to himself, and set before him, the great Love of God. That God willeth not the Death of a Sinner, but that he repent and believe; that Christ calleth poor Sinners very kindly and graciously to Himself, and will refresh them; that God hath sent His Son into the World, to seek and save that which is lost, viz. the poor repentant and returning Sinner; and that for the poor Sinner's Sake He hath given His Life unto Death, and died for him in our Humanity which He took upon Him.

Furthermore, he must firmly persuade himself that God in Christ Jesus will much more readily hear him and receive him to Grace, than he will readily come; and that God in the Love of

Christ, in the most dear and precious Name JESUS, cannot will any Evil. That there is no angry Countenance at all in this Name, but that It is the highest and deepest Love and Faithfulness, the greatest Sweetness of the Deity, in the great Name JEHOVAH, which He has manifested in our Humanity, corrupted as it is, and perished as to the Heavenly Part, which in Paradise disappeared through Sin. And He was therefore moved in His Heart to flow into us with His Sweet Love, that the Anger of His Father, which was kindled in us, might be quenched and turned into Love by It. All which was done for the poor Sinner's Sake, that he might obtain an open Gate of Grace again.

In this Consideration he must firmly imagine to himself that this very Hour and Instant he standeth before the Face of the Holy Trinity, and that God is really present within and without him, as the Holy Scripture witnesseth, saying, Am not I He that filleth all Things? And in another Place, The Word is near thee, in thy Mouth, and in thy Heart. Also, We will come unto you and make Our abode with you. And, Behold, I am with you always, even to the End of the World. And again, The Kingdom of God is within you.

Thus he must firmly know and believe, that with, and in his Interior he standeth really before the Face of Jesus Christ, even before the Holy Deity, on whom his Soul hath turned its Back; and must resolve that he will this very Hour turn the Eyes and Desire of his Soul towards God again, and with the poor, lost, and returning Son, come to the Father. He must, with the Eyes of his Mind cast down in Fear and deepest Humility, begin to confess his Sins and Unworthiness before the Face of God in manner following:

A short Form of Confession before the Face of God

Everyone, as his Case and Necessity requires, may order and enlarge this Confession as the Holy Ghost shall teach him. I will only set down a short Direction.

O Thou great unsearchable GOD, LORD of all Things; Thou, Who in Christ Jesus, of great Love towards us, hath manifested Thyself with Thy holy Substance in our Humanity: I, poor unworthy sinful Wretch, come before Thy Presence, which Thou hast manifested in the Humanity of Jesus Christ, though I am not worthy to lift up mine Eyes to Thee, acknowledging and confessing before Thee, that I am guilty of Unfaithfulness, and Breaking off from Thy great Love and Grace, which Thou hast freely bestowed upon us. I have left the Covenant, which of mere Grace Thou hast made with me in Baptism, in which Thou didst receive me to be a Child and Heir of Eternal Life, and I have brought my Desire into the Vanity of this World, and defiled by Soul therewith, and made it altogether beastial and earthly. So that my Soul knoweth not itself, because of the Mire of Sin; but accounteth itself a strange Child before Thy Face, not worthy to desire Thy Grace. I lie in the Guilt and Filth of Sin, and the Vanity of my corrupt Flesh, up to the very Lips of my Soul, and have but a small Spark of the living Breath left in me, which desireth Thy Grace. I am dead in Sin and Corruption, so that in this woeful Condition I dare not lift up mine Eyes to Thee.

O God in Christ Jesus, Thou who for poor Sinners' Sakes didst become Man to help them, to Thee I complain; to Thee I have yet a Spark of Refuge in my Soul. I have not regarded Thy purchased Inheritance, which Thou hast purchased for us poor Men, by Thy bitter Death, but have made myself a Partaker of the Heritage of Vanity, in the Anger of my Father in the Curse of the Earth, and am ensnared in Sin, and half dead as to Thy Kingdom. I lie in Feebleness as to Thy Strength, and the wrathful Death waiteth for me. The Devil hath poisoned me, so that I know not my Saviour: I am become a wild Branch on Thy Tree, and have consumed mine Inheritance which is in Thee, with the Devil's Swine. What shall I say before Thee, who am not worthy of Thy Grace? I lie in the Sleep of Death which hath captivated me, and am fast Bound with three strong Chains. O Thou Breaker-through-Death, assist me, I beseech Thee; I cannot, I am able to do nothing! I am dead in myself, and have no Strength before Thee, neither dare I, for great Shame, lift up mine Eyes unto Thee. For I am the defiled Keeper of Swine, and have spent mine Inheritance with the false adulterous Whore of Vanity in the Lusts of the Flesh; I have sought myself in my own Lust, and not Thee. Now in myself I am become a Fool; I am naked and bare; my Shame stands before mine Eyes; I cannot hide it; Thy Judgement waiteth for me. What shall I say before Thee, Who art the Judge of all the World? I have nothing to bring before Thee. - Here I stand naked and bare in Thy Presence, and fall down before Thy Face bewailing my Misery, and fly to Thy great Mercy, though I am not worthy of It; yet receive me but in Thy Death, and let me but die from my Death in Thine. Cast me down, I pray Thee, to the Ground in my innate SELF, and kill this SELF of mine through Thy Death, that I may live no more to mySELF, seeing I in mySELF work nothing but Sin. Therefore, I pray Thee, cast down to the Ground this wicked Beast, which is full of false Deceit and SELF-Desire, and deliver this poor Soul of mine from its heavy Bonds.

O merciful God, it is owing to Thy Love and Long-Suffering that I lie not already in Hell. I yield my SELF, with my whole Will, Senses and Mind, unto Thy Grace, and fly to Thy Mercy. I call upon Thee through Thy Death, from that small Spark of Life in me encompassed with Death and Hell, which open their Throat against me, and would wholly swallow me up in Death; upon Thee I call, Who hast promised that Thou wilt not quench the smoking Flax. I have no other Way to Thee but by Thy Own bitter Death and Passion, because Thou hast made our Death to be Life by Thy Humanity, and broken the Chains of Death, and therefore I sink the Desire of my Soul down into Thy Death, into the Gate of Thy Death, which Thou hast broke open.

O Thou great Fountain of the Love of God, I beseech Thee, help me, that I may die from my Vanity and Sin in the Death of my Redeemer, Jesus Christ.

O Thou Breath of the great Love of God, quicken, I beseech Thee, my weak Breath in me, that it may begin to hunger and thirst after Thee. O Lord Jesus, Thou sweet Strength, I beseech Thee give my Soul to drink of Thy Fountain of Grace, Thy sweet Water of Eternal Life, that it may awake from Death and thirst after Thee. O how extreme fainting I am for Want of Thy Strength! O merciful God, do Thou turn me, I beseech Thee; I cannot turn myself. O Thou Vanquisher of Death, help me, I pray Thee, to wrestle. How fast doth the Enemy hold me with his three Chains, and will not suffer the Desire of my Soul to come before Thee! I beseech Thee, come and take the Desire of my Soul into Thyself. Be Thou my Drawing to the Father, and deliver me from the Devil's Bonds! Look not upon my Deformity in standing naked before Thee, having lost Thy Garment! I pray Thee, do but Thou clothe that Breath which yet liveth in me and panteth after Thy Grace; and so shall I yet see Thy Salvation.

O Thou deep Love, I pray Thee take the Desire of my Soul into Thee; bring it forth out of the Bonds of Death through Thy Death, in Thy Resurrection, into Thee. O quicken me in Thy Strength, that my Desire and Will may begin to spring up and flourish anew. O Thou Vanquisher of Death and of the Wrath of God, do Thou overcome SELF in me; break its Will and bruise my Soul, that it may fear before Thee, and be ashamed of its OWN Will before Thy Judgement, and that it may be ever obedient to Thee as an Instrument of Thine. Subdue it in the Bonds of Death; take away its Power, that it may will nothing without Thee.

O God, the Holy Ghost in Christ my Saviour, teach me, I pray Thee, what I shall do, that I may turn to Thee. O draw me in Christ to the Father, and help me, that now and from henceforward I may go forth from Sin and Vanity, and never any more enter into them again. Stir up in me a true Sorrow for the Sins I have committed. O keep me in Thy Bonds; and let me not loose from Thee, lest the Devil sift me in my wicked Flesh and Blood, and bring me again into the Death of Death. O enlighten Thou my Spirit, that I may see the Divine Path, and walk in it continually. O take that away from me, which always turneth me away from Thee; and give me that which always turneth me to

Thee; take me wholly from MySELF and give me wholly to THYself. O let me begin nothing, let me will, think, and do nothing without Thee. O Lord, how long! Indeed I am not worthy of that which I desire of Thee, I pray Thee let the Desire of my Soul dwell but in the Gates of Thy Courts; make it but a Servant of Thy Servants. O preserve it from that horrible Pit, wherein there is no Comfort or Refreshment.

O God in Christ Jesus! I am blind in my SELF, and know not myself because of Vanity. Thou art hidden from me in my Blindness, and yet Thou art near unto me; but Thy Wrath which my Desire hath awakened in me, hath made me dark. O take but the Desire of my Soul to Thee; prove it, O Lord, and bruise it, that my Soul may obtain a Ray of Thy Sweet Grace.

I lie before Thee as a dying Man, whose Life is passing from his Lips, as a small Spark going out; kindle it, O Lord, and raise up the Breath of my Soul before Thee. Lord, I wait for Thy Promise, which Thou hast made, saying, As I live, I will not the Death of a Sinner, but that he shall turn and live. I sink myself down into the Death of my Redeemer, Jesus Christ, and wait for Thee, whose Word is Truth and Life. Amen.

In this, or the like Manner, every one may confess his Sins, as he himself findeth on examining his Conscience, what Sins he hath brought his Soul into. Yet if his Purpose be truly earnest, to use a Form is needless, for the Spirit of God, which at that Instant is in the Will of the Mind, will Itself make the Prayer for him, in his Interior. For it is the Spirit of God, which in a true earnest Desire worketh Repentance, and intercedeth for the Soul before God, through the Death of Christ.

But I will not hide from the beloved Reader, who hath a True Christian Intent, how it commonly goeth with those who are in such a firm Purpose and Resolution; though, indeed, it goeth otherwise with one than with another, according as his Purpose is more or less earnest and strong. For the Spirit of God is not bound, but useth diverse Ways or Processes accordingly as He knoweth to be fittest for every one. Yet a Soldier who hath been in the Wars can tell how to fight and instruct another that may happen to be in the like Condition.

Now when such a Heart with strong Resolution and Purpose doth thus come before God, and enter into Repentance, it happeneth to it as to the Canaanitish Woman; that is, it seems as if God would not hear. The Heart remaineth without Comfort as its Sins, Follies, and Neglects also present themselves to it, and make it feel itself unworthy of any. The Mind is as it were speechless; the Soul groaneth in the Deep; the Heart receiveth nothing, nor can it so much as pour forth its Confession before God; but it is as if the Heart and Soul were quite shut up. The Soul would fain go towards God, but the Flesh keepeth it captive: The Devil too shuteth it up strongly, and representeth to it the Way of Vanity again, and tickleth it with the Lust of the Flesh, and saith inwardly to it, Stay a while, do this or that first; get a Sufficiency of Money or Goods beforehand, that thou mayest not stand in Need of the World, and afterwards enter into Repentance and a Holy Life; it will be Time enough then.

O how many Hundreds perish in such a Beginning, if they go back again into Vanity; and become as young Grafts broken off by the Wind, or withered by the Heat!

Beloved Soul, mark: If thou wilt be a Champion in thy Saviour Christ against Death and Hell, and wouldst have thy young Graft grow, and become a Tree in the Kingdom of Christ, thou must go on, and stand fast in thy first earnest Purpose. It is as much as thy paternal Inheritance is worth, and thy Body and Soul too, whether thou, becomest an Angel in God, or a Devil in Hell. If thou wilt be crowned, thou must fight; thou must overcome in Christ, and not yield to the Devil. Thy Purpose must stand firm, thou must not prefer temporal Honor and Goods before It. When the Spirit of the Flesh says, Stay a while, it is not convenient yet; then the Soul must say, Now is the Time for me to go back again into my Native Country, out of which my Father, Adam, hath brought me. No Creature shall keep me back, and though thou earthly Body shouldest thereby decay and perish, yet I will now enter with my Will and whole Desire, into the Rose-

Garden of my Redeemer, Jesus Christ; through His Suffering and Death into Him, and in the Death of Christ subdue thee, thou earthly Body, that hast swallowed up my Pearl from me, which God gave to my Father, Adam in Paradise. I will break the Will of thy Voluptuousness, which is in Vanity, and bind thee as a mad Dog with the Chain of my earnest Purpose; and though hereby thou shouldest become a Fool in the Account of all Men, yet thou must and shalt obey the firm Resolve of my Soul. Nothing shall unloose thee from this Chain, but the temporal Death. Whereunto God and his Strength help me.

A short Direction how the poor Soul must come before God again, and how it must fight for the Noble Garland; what Kind of Weapons it must use, if it will go to War against God's Anger, against the Devil, the World and Sin, against Flesh and Blood, against the Influence of the Stars and Elements, and all its other Enemies.

BELOVED Soul, there is Earnestness required to do this, and not a bare Recital of Words only! No, the earnest resolved Will must drive on this Work, else nothing will be effected. For if the Soul will obtain the triumphant Garland of Christ from the noble Sophia or Divine Wisdom, it must wooe Her for it in great Desire of Love. It must entreat Her in Her most Holy Name for It, and come before Her in most modest Humility, and not like a lustful Bull or a wanton Venus. For so long as any are such, they must not seek these Things; for they shall not obtain them, and though something should be obtained by those who are in such an impure State, it would be no more than a Glimpse of the true Glory. But a chaste and modest Mind may prevail so far as to have the Soul in its noble Image, which died in Adam, quickened in the Heavenly Corporality as to the inward Ground, and the precious Garland set upon it. Yet if this should come to pass, It is taken off again from the Soul, and laid by, as a Crown useth to be, after a King is once crowned with it; it is then laid by and kept. So it cometh to pass also with the Heavenly Garland or Gift. It is taken from the Soul again, because the Soul is yet encompassed with the House of Sin; so that if it should unhappily fall again, its

Crown might not be defiled. This is spoken plainly enough for the Children that know and have tried these Things: None of the Wicked are worthy to know more about them.

The Process, or WAY

A Man must bring a serious Mind to this Work. He must come before God with sincere Earnestness, deep Humility, and hearty Sorrow for his Sins, and with a deliberate and firm Resolution, not to enter any more into the old broad Way of Vanity. And though the whole World should account him a Fool, and he should lose both Honor and Goods, nay, and the temporal Life also, for the Sake of his new Choice, yet he must resolve firmly to abide by it.

If ever he will obtain the Love and Marriage of the noble Sophia, he must make such a Vow as this in his Purpose and Mind. For Christ Himself saith, He that forsaketh not Wife and Children, Brethren and Sisters, Money and Goods, and all that he hath, and even his earthly Life also, to follow Me, is not worthy of Me. Here Christ meaneth the Mind of the Soul, so that if there were any Thing that would keep the Mind back from It, though it should have never so fair and glorious a Pretence or Show in this World, the Mind must not regard it at all, but rather part with it than with the Love of the noble Virgin Sophia, in the Bud and Blossom of Christ, in His tender Humanity in us as to the Heavenly Corporality. For this is the Flower in Sharon, the Rose in the Valley of Jericho, wherewith Solomon delighted himself, and termed it his dear Love, his chaste Virgin which he loved; as indeed all other Saints before and after him did; whosoever obtained Her, called Her his Pearl.

After what Manner to pray for It, you may see by this short Direction following. The Work itself must be committed to the Holy Ghost; He formeth and frameth the Prayer for the Soul, in every Heart wherein He is sought.

The PRAYER

I, a poor unworthy Creature, come before Thee, O Great and Holy God and lift up mine eyes to Thee. Though I am not worthy, yet Thy great Mercy, and Thy faithful Promise in the Word, have now encouraged me to lift the Eyes of the Desire of my Soul up to Thee. For my Soul hath now laid hold on the Word of Thy Promise, and received It into itself, and therewith cometh to Thee. And though it is but a strange Child which was disobedient unto Thee, yet now it desireth to be obedient; and doth now infold itself with its Desire into that Word which became Man, which became Flesh and Blood, and hath broken Sin and Death in my Humanity. Which hath changed the Anger of God into Love unto the Soul, hath deprived Death of his Power, and Hell of its Victory over Soul and Body; and hath opened a Gate for my Soul to the clear Face of Thy Strength and Power.

O Great and Most Holy God, I have brought the Hunger and Desire of my Soul into this most Holy Word, and now I come before Thee, and in my Hunger call unto Thee, Thou living Fountain, through Thy Word which became Flesh and Blood. Thy Word being made the Life in our Flesh, I receive It firmly into the Desire of my Soul as my own Life; and I pierce into Thee with the Desire of my Soul through the Word in the Flesh of Christ; through His holy Conception in the Virgin Mary, His Incarnation, His holy Nativity, His Baptism in the Jordan, His Temptation in the Wilderness - where He overcame the Kingdom of the Devil and this World in the Humanity. Through all His Miracles, which He did on Earth; through His Reproach and Ignominy, His innocent Death and Passion, the Shedding of His Blood, wherein God's Anger in Soul and Flesh was drowned. Through His Rest in the Sepulchre, when He awaked our Father Adam out of his Sleep, who was fallen into a dead Sleep as to the Kingdom of Heaven. Through His Love, which pierced through the Anger and destroyed Hell in the Soul. Through His Resurrection from the Dead, His Ascension, the Sending of the

Holy Spirit into our Soul and Spirit, and through all His Promises; one of which is, that Thou, O God the Father, wilt give the Holy Spirit to them that ask It, in the Name and through the Word which became Man.

O Thou Life of my Flesh and of my Soul in Christ my Brother, I beseech Thee in the Hunger of my Soul, and entreat Thee with all my Powers, though they be weak, to give me what Thou hast promised me, and freely bestow upon me in my Saviour Jesus Christ, His Flesh for Food, and His Blood for Drink, to refresh my poor hungry Soul, that it may be quickened and strengthened in the Word which became Man, by which it may long and hunger after Thee aright.

O Thou deepest Love in the most Sweet Name JESUS, give Thyself into the Desire of my Soul. For therefore Thou hast moved Thyself, and according to Thy great Sweetness manifested Thyself in the Human Nature, and called us to Thee, us that hunger and thirst after Thee, and hast promised us that Thou wilt refresh us. I now open the lips of my Soul to Thee, O Thou Sweet Truth, and though I am not worthy to desire it of Thy Holiness, yet I come to Thee through Thy bitter Passion and Death; Thou having sprinkled my Uncleanness with Thy Blood, and sanctified me in Thy Humanity, and made an open Gate for me through Thy Death, to Thy Sweet Love in Thy Blood. Through Thy five holy Wounds, from which Thou didst shed Thy Blood, I bring the Desire of my Soul into Thy Love.

O Jesus Christ, thou Son of God and Man, I pray Thee receive into Thyself Thy purchased Inheritance, which Thy Father hath given Thee. I cry within me, that I may enter through Thy Holy Blood and Death into Thee. Open Thyself in me, that the Spirit of my Soul may reach Thee, and receive Thee into it. Lay hold on my Thirst in me with Thy Thirst; bring Thy Thirst after us Men, which Thou hadst upon the Cross, into my Thirst, and give me Thy Blood to drink in my Thirst. That my Death in me which holdeth me captive, may be drowned in the Blood of Thy Love, and that my extinguished or suppressed Image, which as to the Kingdom of Heaven disappeared in my Father Adam through Sin, may be made alive through Thy powerful Blood, and my Soul clothed with It again as with the new Body which dwelleth in Heaven. In which Image Thy Holy Power and Word that became Man dwelleth, which is the Temple of the Holy Spirit, Who dwelleth in us according to Thy Promise, saying We will come to you and make Our Abode with you.

O Thou Great Love of Jesus Christ, I can do no more than sink my Desire into Thee; Thy Word which became Man, is Truth; since Thou hast bidden me come, now I come. Be it unto me according to Thy Word and Will. Amen.

A Warning to the Reader

Beloved Reader, out of Love to thee, I will not conceal from thee what is here earnestly signified to me. If thou lovest the Vanity of the Flesh still, and art not in an earnest Purpose on the WAY to the new Birth or Regeneration, intending to become a New Man, then leave the above-written Words un-named; else they will turn to a Judgement of God in thee. Thou must not take the Holy Names in vain, thou art faithfully warned: They belong to the thirsty Soul. But if thy Soul be in earnest, it shall find by Experience what Words they are.

A Direction how the Soul must meet its Beloved, when She knocketh in its Center, or Shut-Inner-Chamber

Beloved Soul, if thou wilt be earnest without Intermission, thou shalt certainly obtain the Favor of a Kiss from the Noble Sophia (or Divine Wisdom) in the Holy Name JESUS; for She standeth ever before the Door of the Soul, knocking, and warning the Sinner of his wicked Way. Now if it once thus desireth Her Love, She is ready for it and kisseth it with the Beams of Her Sweet Love, from whence the Heart receiveth Joy. But She doth not presently lay Herself in the Marriage-Bed with the Soul, that is, She doth not presently awaken the extinguished Heavenly Image in Herself, which disappeared in Adam in Paradise. No, there might be Danger to Man in that; for if Adam and Lucifer fell, having it manifested in them, the same may easily happen to Man, who is still so strongly enthralled in Vanity.

The Bond of thy Promise must be firm and steadfast. Before She will crown thee, thou must be tempted and tried: She taketh the Beams of Her Love from thee again, to see whether thou wilt prove faithful; also She letteth thee stand as it were aloof, and answereth thee not so much as with one Look of Her Love. For before She will crown thee, thou must be judged, that thou mayest taste the bitter Potion of Dregs, which thou hast filled for thyself in thine Abominations. Thou must come before the Gates of Hell first, and there show forth thy Victory for Her in Her Love, in that Strength wherewith She upheld thee in Opposition to the Devil's malign influence.

Christ was tempted in the Wilderness; and if thou wilt put on Him, thou must go through His whole Progress or Journey, even from His Incarnation to His Ascension. And though thou art not able, nor required to do that which He hath done; yet thou must enter wholly into His Process, and therein die continually from the Corruption of the Soul. For the Virgin Sophia espouseth not Herself to the Soul, except in this Property, which springeth up in the Soul through the Death of Christ, as a new Plant standing in Heaven. The earthly Body cannot comprehend Her in this Life-time, for it must first die from the corruptible Vanity; but the Heavenly Image which disappeared in Adam, viz. the true Seed of the Woman, wherein God became Man, and into which He brought His living Seed, the Heavenly Substantiality, is capable of the Pearl, after the Manner wherein it came to pass in Mary, in the End or Fulfilling of the Covenant.

Therefore take heed what thou doest. When thou hast made thy Promise, keep it, and then She will crown thee more readily than thou wouldst be crowned. But thou must be sure when the Tempter cometh to thee with the Pleasure, Beauty, and Glory of the World, that thy Mind reject it, and say, I must be a Servant and not a Master in the Vineyard of Christ; I am but a Steward of God in and over all that I have, and I must do with it as His

Word teacheth me; my Heart must sit down with the simple and lowly, in the Dust, and be always humble. Whatsoever State and Condition thou art in, Humility must be in the Front, or else thou wilt not obtain the Noble Virgin in Marriage. The Free Will of thy Soul must stand the Brunt as a Champion; for if the Devil cannot prevail against the Soul with Vanity, nor catch it with that Bait, then he cometh with its Unworthiness and Catalogue of Sins. And there thou must fight hard, and the Merits of Christ must be set in the Front, or else the Creature cannot prevail against the Devil. For in this Conflict it goeth so terribly with many a poor Sinner, that outward Reason thinketh him to be distracted, or possessed by an evil Spirit. The Devil defendeth himself so horribly in some, especially if he hath had a great Fort of Prey in them, that he must be stoutly assaulted before he will depart and leave his Castle. In this kind of Combat, Heaven and Hell are fighting one against the other.

Now if the Soul continue constant, and getteth the Victory over the Devil in all his Assaults, disesteeming all temporal Things for the Love of its Noble Sophia, then the precious Garland will be set upon it for a Token or Ensign of Victory.

Here the Virgin, (which manifesteth Herself in the dear Name of JESUS CHRIST, the Treader upon the Serpent, God's Anointed) cometh to the Soul, and kisseth it with Her Sweetest Love in the Essence most inwardly, and impresseth Her Love into its Desire for a Token of Victory. And here Adam in his Heavenly Part riseth again from Death in Christ. Of which I cannot write; for there is no Pen in this World that can express it: It is the Wedding of the Lamb where the Noble Pearl is sown with very great Triumph; though in the beginning it be small as a Grain of Mustard-Seed, as Christ saith.

Now when the Wedding is over, the Soul must take heed that this Pearl-Tree, or Tree of Faith spring and grow, as it hath promised the Virgin; for then the Devil will presently come with his furious Storm, the ungodly People, who will scoff at, contemn, and cry down this WAY for Madness; and then a Man must enter into the Process of Christ, under his Cross. Here it will appear indeed and in Truth, what Sort of a Christian he is. For he must suffer himself to be proclaimed a Fool and ungodly Wretch; nay, his greatest Friends, who favored him, or flattered him in the Lusts of the Flesh, will now be his Enemies, and though they know not why, will hate him. Thus it is that Christ hideth his Bride wholly under the Cross, that she may not be known in this World: The Devil also striveth that these Children may be hidden from the World, lest haply many such Branches should grow in the Garden which he supposeth to be his.

This I have set down for the Information of the Christian-minded Reader, that he may know what to do, if the same should befall him.

A very earnest Prayer in Temptation

Against God's Anger in the Conscience; and also against Flesh and Blood, when the Temptation cometh to the Soul, and wrestleth with it.

Most Deep Love of God in Christ Jesus, leave me not in this Distress. I confess I am guilty of the Sins which now rise up in my Mind and Conscience; and if Thou forsake me, I must perish. But hast Thou not promised me in Thy Word, saying, If a Mother could forget her Child, which can hardly be, yet Thou wilt not forget me? Thou hast set me as a Sign in Thine Hands, which were pierced through with sharp Nails, and in Thy open Side whence Blood and Water gushed out. Poor Wretch that I am! I am caught in Thy Anger, and can in my Ability do nothing before Thee; I sink myself down into Thy Wounds and Death.

O Great Mercy of God, I beseech Thee, deliver me from the Bonds of Satan. I have no Refuge in any Thing, but only in Thy Holy Wounds and Death! Into Thee I sink down in the Anguish of my Conscience; do with me what Thou wilt. In Thee I will now live or die, as pleaseth Thee; let me but die and perish in Thy Death; do but bury me into Thy Death, that the Anguish of Hell may not touch me. How can I excuse myself before Thee, that knoweth my Heart and Reins, and settest my Sins before mine Eyes? I am guilty of them, and yield myself unto Thy Judgement; accomplish Thy Judgement upon me, through the Death of my Redeemer Jesus Christ.

I fly unto Thee, Thou Righteous Judge, through the Anguish of my redeemer Jesus Christ, when He did sweat the bloody Sweat on the Mount of Olives for my Sake, and was scourged by Pontius Pilate for me, and suffered a Crown of Thorns to be pressed upon His Head, so that His Blood came forth.

O Righteous God, hast Thou not set Him in my Stead? He was innocent, but I guilty, for whom He suffered, wherefore should I despair under Thy Wrath? O blot out Thy Anger in me through His Anguish, Passion and Death; I give myself wholly into His Anguish, Passion and Death; I will stand still in His Anguish and Passion before Thee; do with me what Thou pleasest, only let me not depart from His Anguish. Thou hast freely given me His Anguish, and drowned Thy Wrath in Him: And though I have not accepted it, but am departed from Him and become faithless, yet Thou hast given me this precious Pledge in my Flesh and Blood. For He hath taken my Flesh and Soul upon His heavenly Flesh and Blood, and hath satisfied the Anger in my Flesh and Soul in Him, with His Heavenly Blood. Therefore receive me now in His Satisfaction, and put His Anguish, Passion and Death in Thy Wrath, which is kindled in me, and break Thy Judgement in me in the Blood of His Love.

O Great Love! in the Blood and Death of Jesus Christ, I beseech Thee, break the strong Fort of Prey which the Devil hath made and built up in me, where he resisteth me in the WAY of Thy Grace. Drive him out of me, that he may not overcome me; for no one living can stand in Thy Sight, if Thou withdraw Thy Hand from him.

O come, Thou Breaker-Through the Anger of God, destroy its Power, and help my poor Soul to fight and overcome it. O bring me into Victory, and uphold me in Thee; break in pieces its Seat in my Vanity, that is kindled in my Soul and Flesh. O mortify the Desire of my Vanity in Flesh and Blood, which the

Devil hath now kindled by his false Desire, by hellish Anguish and Desperation. O quench it with Thy Water of Eternal Life, and bring my Anguish forth through Thy Death, I wholly sink myself down into Thee; and though Soul and Body should this hour faint and perish in Thy Wrath, yet I will not let Thee go. Though my Heart saith utterly, No, no, yet the Desire of my Soul shall hold fast on Thy Truth, which neither Death nor the Devil shall take away from me; for the Blood of Jesus Christ, the Son of God, cleanseth us from all our Sins. This I lay hold on, and let the Anger of God do what It will with my Sin, and let the Devil roar over my Soul in his Fort of Prey which he hath made, as much as he will: Neither the Devil, Death, nor Hell shall pull me out of my Saviour's Wounds. Thou must at length be confounded in me, thou malicious Devil, and thy Fort of Prey must be forsaken, for I will drown it in the Love of Jesus Christ, and then dwell in it if thou canst. Amen.

An Information in Temptation

Beloved Reader, this is no jesting Matter; he that accounteth it so, hath not tried it, neither hath he yet passed the Judgement; but his Conscience is still asleep; and though it should be deferred to his latter Days, which is very dangerous, yet he must pass through this Judgement or fiery Trial. Happy is he that passeth through it in the Time of his Youth, before the Devil buildeth his Fort of Prey strong; he may afterwards prove a Labourer in the heavenly Vineyard, and sow his Seed in the Garden of Christ; where he shall reap the Fruit in due Time. This Judgement continueth a long while upon many a poor Soul; several Years, if he doth not earnestly and early put on the Armour of Christ, but stayeth till the Judgement of Tribulation first drive him to Repentance. But to him that cometh by himself, of his own earnest Purpose, and endeavoreth to depart from his evil Ways, the Temptation or Trial will not be so hard, neither will it continue so long. Yet he must stand out valiantly, till Victory be gotten over the Devil; for he shall be mightily assisted, and all shall end in the best for him; so that afterwards when the Day breaketh in his Soul, he turneth it to the great Praise and Glory of God, that his grand Enemy and Persecutor was overcome in the Conflict.

SHORT PRAYERS

When the Noble Sophia (or Eternal Wisdom) kisseth the Soul with Her Love, and offereth Her Love to it

O Most Gracious and Deep Love of God in Christ Jesus! I beseech Thee grant me Thy Pearl, impress It into my Soul, and take my Soul into Thy Arms.

O Thou Sweet Love! I confess I am unclean before Thee. Take away my Uncleanness through Thy Death, and carry the Hunger and Thirst of my Soul through Thy Death in Thy Resurrection, in Thy Triumph! Cast my whole SELF-hood down to the Ground in Thy Death; take it captive, and carry my Hunger through in Thy Hunger.

O Highest Love! Hast Thou not appeared in me? Stay in me, and inclose me in Thee. Keep me in Thee, so that I may not be able to depart from Thee. Fill my Hunger with Thy Love; feed my Soul with Thy Heavenly Substance; give it Thy Blood to drink, and water it with Thy Fountain.

O Great Love! Awaken my disappeared Image in me, which, as to the Kingdom of Heaven disappeared in my Father Adam. By the Word, which awakened the same Image in the Seed of the Woman in Mary; quicken It, I beseech Thee.

O Thou Life and Power of the Deity, Who hast promised us, saying, We will come to you, and make Our Abode in you. O Sweet Love! I bring my Desire into this Word of Thy Promise. Thou hast promised also, that Thy Father will give the Holy Spirit to those that ask Him for It; therefore I now bring the Desire of my Soul into that Thy Promise, and I receive Thy Word into my Hunger. Increase Thou in me my Hunger after Thee. Strengthen me, O sweet Love, in Thy Strength: Quicken me in Thee, that my Spirit may taste Thy Sweetness. O do thou believe by Thy Power in me, for without Thee I can do nothing.

O Sweet Love! I beseech Thee through that Love wherewith Thou didst overcome the Anger of God, and didst change it into Love and Divine Joy; I pray Thee also change the Anger in my Soul by that same great Love, that I may become obedient unto Thee, and that my Soul may love Thee therein forever. O change my Will into Thy Will; bring Thy Obedience into my Disobedience, that I may become obedient unto Thee.

O Great Love of Jesus Christ, I humbly fly to Thee; bring the Hunger of my Soul into Thy Wounds, from whence Thou didst shed Thy Holy Blood, and didst quench the Anger with Love. I bring my Hunger into Thy open Side, from whence came forth Water and Blood, and throw myself wholly into It; be Thou mine, and quicken me in Thy Life, and let me not depart from Thee.

O my Noble Vine, I beseech Thee give Sap to me Thy Branch; that I may bud and grow in Thy Strength and Sap, in Thy Essence; beget in me true Strength by Thy Strength.

O Sweet Love, art Thou not my Light? Enlighten Thou my poor Soul in its close Prison in Flesh and Blood. Bring it into the Right WAY. Destroy the Will of the Devil, and bring my Body through the whole Course of this World, through the Chamber of Death into Thy Death and Rest; that at the Last Day it may arise in Thee from Thy Death, and live in Thee forever. O teach me what I must do in Thee; I beseech Thee be Thou my Willing, Knowing, and Doing; and let me go no whither without Thee. I yield myself wholly up to Thee. Amen.

A PRAYER

For obtaining the Divine Working, Protection, and Government; showing also how the Mind should work with and in God, in Christ the Tree of Life

O Thou living Fountain, in Thee I lift up the Desire of my Soul, and cry with my Desire to enter through the Life of my Saviour Jesus Christ into Thee.

O Thou Life and Power of God, awaken Thyself in the Hunger of my Soul with Thy Desire of Love, through the Thirst which Jesus Christ had upon the Cross after us Men, and carry my weak Strength through by Thy mighty Hand in Thy Spirit; be Thou the Working and Will in me with Thine own Strength. Blossom in the Strength of Jesus Christ in me, that I may bring forth Praise unto Thee, the true Fruit of Thy Kingdom. O let my Heart and Desire never depart from Thee more.

But I swim in Vanity in this Valley of Misery, in this outward earthly Flesh and Blood; and my Soul and Noble Image, which is according to Thy Similitude, is encompassed with Enemies on every Side; with the Desire of the Devil against me, with the Desire of Vanity in Flesh and Blood; also with all the Opposition of wicked Men who know not Thy Name. And I swim with my outward Life in the Properties of the Stars and Elements, having my Enemies lying in wait for me everywhere, inwardly and outwardly, together with Death the Destroyer of this vain Life. I fly therefore to Thee, O Holy Strength of God, seeing Thou hast manifested Thyself with Thy loving Mercy in our Humanity, through Thy Holy Name JESUS, and hast also given It to be a Companion and Guide in us. I beseech Thee let His Angels that minister to Him, attend upon the Souls of me and mine, and encamp themselves about us, and defend us from the fiery Darts of the Desire of that wicked One, which he shooteth into us daily by the Curse of the Anger of God which is awakened in our earthly Flesh. Keep back by Thy Divine Strength the malignant Influence of the Stars in their Opposition, wherein the wicked Enemy of Mankind mingleth himself with his Desire and Imagination, in order to poison us in Soul and Flesh, and to bring us into false and evil Desires, as also into Infirmity and Misery. Turn away these evil Influences by Thy Holy Power Jesus, from our Souls and Spirits, that they may not touch us; and let Thy Good and Holy Angels stand by us to turn away their noxious Effects from our Bodies.

O Great Love and Sweet Strength JESU, Thou Fountain of Divine Sweetness, flowing out of the great Eternal Name JEHOVAH, I cry with the Desire of my Soul to come into Thee. My Soul cryeth to come into that Spirit, from Which it was breathed into the Body, and Which hath formed it in the Likeness of God. It desireth in its Thirst to get the Sweet Fountain which springeth from JEHOVAH into itself, to refresh God's Breath of Fire, which itself is, that so the Sweet Love of JESUS may rise in its Breath of Fire, through the Fountain JESUS springing out of JEHOVAH; that CHRIST the Holy One may be manifested, and become Man in my disappeared Image of Heavenly Spiritual Corporality, and that my poor Soul may receive its beloved Bride again into its Arms, with whom it may rejoice forever.

O IMMANUEL! thou Wedding-Chamber, God and Man, I yield myself up into the Arms of Thy Desire towards us, in us; it is Thyself whom I desire. O blot out the Anger of Thy Father with Thy Love in me, and manifest Thy Strength in my Weakness, that I may overcome and tame the Evil of Flesh and Blood, and serve Thee in Holiness and Righteousness.

O Thou Great and Most Holy Name and Majesty of God, JEHOVAH, Which hast stirred Thyself with Thy Most Sweet Power JESUS, in the Limit of the covenanted Promise to our Father Adam, in the Woman's Seed; in the Virgin Mary, in our disappeared Heavenly Humanity, and brought the living Essentiality of Thy Holy Power in the Virgin Wisdom of God into our Humanity, which was extinguished as to Thee; and hast given It to us, to be our Life, Regeneration, and Victory; I entreat Thee with all my Strength, beget a new Holy Life in me, by Thy

Sweet Power JESUS, that I may be in Thee and Thou in me; that so Thy Kingdom may be made manifest in me, and the Will and Conversation of my Soul may be in Heaven.

O Great and Incomprehensible God, thou who fillest all Things, be Thou my Heaven in which my new Birth of Christ Jesus may dwell: Let my Spirit be the stringed Instrument, Harmony, Sound and Joy of Thy Holy Spirit. Strike the Strings in me in Thy Regenerate Image, and carry through my Harmony into Thy Divine Kingdom of Joy, in the Great Love of God, in the Wonders of Thy Glory and Majesty, in the Communion of the Holy Angelical Harmony. Build up the Holy City Zion in me, in which as Children of Christ we all live together in one City, which is Christ in us. Into Thee I wholly plunge myself; do with me what Thou pleasest. Amen.

A PRAYER

To be used by a Soul in Tribulation under the Cross of Christ, when it is assaulted by its outward Enemies, who persecute and hate it for being in the Spirit of Christ, and slander and reproach it as an Evil-Doer.

Poor Man that I am! I walk full of Anguish and Trouble in my Return towards my Native Country, from whence I wandered in Adam, and am going back again through the Thistles and Thorns of this troublesome World. O God my Father, the Briars tear me on every Side, and I am afflicted and despised by my Enemies. They scorn my Soul, and revile it as an Evil-Doer, who hath broken Faith with them; they deride my walking towards Thee, and account it foolish. They think I am senseless, because I walk in this straight and thorny Path, and go not along with them in their hypocritical broad Way.

O Lord JESUS CHRIST, I fly to Thee under the Cross; O dear Immanuel receive me, and carry me into Thyself through the Path of Thy Pilgrimage, in which Thou didst walk in this World, namely through Thy Incarnation, Poverty, Reproach, and Scorn;

also through Thy Anguish, Passion, and Death. Make me conformable unto Thy Example; send Thy good Angel along with me, to show me the WAY through the horrible thorny Wilderness of this World. Assist me in my Misery; comfort me with that Comfort wherewith the Angel comforted Thee in the Garden, when Thou didst pray to Thy Father, and didst sweat great Drops of Blood. Support me in my Anguish and Persecution, under the Reproach of the Devils, and all wicked Men, who know not Thee, and refuse to walk in Thy Paths. O great Love of God, they know not Thy Way, and do this in Blindness, through the Deceit of the Devil. Have Pity on them, and bring them out of their Darkness into Thy Light, that they may learn to know themselves, and how they lie Captive in the Filth and Mire of the Devil, in a dark Dungeon fast bound with three Chains. O Great God have Mercy upon Adam and his Children, redeem them in Christ, the new Adam.

I fly to Thee, O Christ, God and Man, in this Pilgrimage and Journey which I must take through this dark Valley, despised and troubled on all Sides, and accounted an ungodly wicked Man. O Lord, it is Thy Judgement upon me, that my Sins and inbred Corruption may be judged in this earthly Pilgrimage before Thee; and I, as a Curse, be made an open Spectacle on which Thy Anger may satiate itself, and thereby may take the eternal Reproach away from me. It is the Token of Thy Love, by which Thou bringest me into the Reproach, Anguish, Suffering, and Death of my Saviour Jesus Christ, that so I may die from Vanity and spring up in His Spirit with a new Life, through His Reproach, Ignominy, and Death.

I beseech Thee, O Christ, Thou patient Lamb of God, grant me Patience in this my WAY of the Cross, through all Thy Anguish and Reproach, thy Death and Passion, Thy Scorn and Contempt upon the Cross, where Thou was despised in my Stead; and bring me therein as a patient Lamb to Thee, into Thy Victory. Let me live with Thee in Thee; and do Thou convert my Persecutors, who (unknown to themselves) by their Reproaching sacrifice my Vanity and inbred Sins before Thy Anger. They know not what they do; they think they do me Harm, but they do me Good! They do that for me which I should do myself before Thee; for I should daily lay open and acknowledge my Shame and Vileness before Thee; and thereby sink myself down into the Death of Thy beloved Son, that my Shame might die in His Death; but I being too negligent, weary, faint, and feeble, therefore Thou usest these mine Enemies in Thine Anger, to open and discover my Vileness before Thee, which Thy Wrath taketh hold of, and sinketh it down into the Death of my Saviour.

O merciful God, my vain Flesh cannot know how well Thou intendest towards me, when Thou sufferest mine Enemies to take my Vileness from me, and sacrifice it before Thee. My earthly Mind supposeth that Thou afflictest me for my Sins, and I am extremely perplexed at it; but Thy Spirit, in my inward new Man, telleth me that it is of Thy Love towards me, and that Thou intendest Good to me by it. When Thou sufferest my Enemies to persecute me, it is best for me that they perform the Work in my Stead, and unfold my Sins before Thee in Thy Anger, that it may swallow up the Guilt of them, so that they may not follow me into my Native Country; for mine Enemies are strong and mighty still in Thy Anger, and therefore can do it better than I that am feeble and fainting already in the Will of Vanity. This Thou knowest full well, O Thou Righteous God.

I beseech Thee therefore, O Righteous God, since Thou usest them as Friends to me, to do so good an Office for me, though my earthly Reason knoweth it not, that Thou wouldst make them also to understand and follow my Course, and send them such Friends in turn; but first bring them to the Light, that they may know Thee, and give Thee Thanks.

O Merciful God in Christ Jesus, I beseech Thee out of Thy deep Love towards us poor Men, which Thou hast manifested in me in the hidden Man, call us all in Thee, to Thee. O stir Thyself in us yet once again in this last Trouble; Thy Anger being kindled in us, do Thou resist it, lest it swallow us up wholly both Soul and Body.

O thou Dawning of the Day-Spring of God, break forth to the Full! Art Thou not already risen? Manifest Thy Holy City Zion, Thy Holy Jerusalem, in us.

O Great God! I see Thee in the Depth of Thy Power and Strength. Awaken me wholly in Thee, that I may be quickened in Thee. Break off the Tree of Thy Anger in us, and let Thy Love spring forth and bud in us.

O Lord, I lie down in Thy Sight, and beseech Thee not to rebuke us in Thine Anger. Are we not Thy Possession which thou hast purchased? Forgive all of us our Sins, and deliver us from the Evil of Thy Wrath, and from the Malice and Envy of the Devil; and bring us under Thy Cross in Patience into Paradise again. Amen.

Here followeth a Prayer or Dialogue between the poor Soul and the Noble Virgin Sophia, in the inward Ground of Man, viz. between the Soul and the Spirit of Christ in the New Birth, out of His Humanity in us; showing how great a Joy there is in the Heaven of the New regenerate Man; and how lovingly and graciously the Noble Sophia presenteth Herself to Her Bridegroom, the Soul, when it entereth into Repentance, and how the Soul behaveth itself towards Her, when She appeareth to it.

The Gates of the Paradisical Garden of Roses

This is understood by none but the Children of Christ, who have known it by Experience.

WHEN Christ the Corner-Stone stirreth Himself in the extinguished Image of Man, in his hearty Conversion and Repentance, then Virgin Sophia appeareth in the Stirring of the Spirit of Christ in the extinguished Image, in Her Virgin's Attire before the Soul; at which the Soul is so amazed and astonished in its Uncleanness, that all its Sins immediately awake in it, and it trembleth before Her; for then the Judgement passeth upon the Sins of the Soul, so that it even goeth back in its Unworthiness, being ashamed in the Presence of its fair Love, and entereth into itself, feeling and acknowledging itself utterly unworthy to receive such a Jewel. This is understood by those who are of our Tribe, and have tasted of this Heavenly Gift, and by none else. But the Noble Sophia draweth near in the Essence of the Soul, and kisseth it in friendly Manner, and tinctureth its dark Fire with Her Rays of Love, and shineth through it with Her bright and powerful Influence. Penetrated with the strong Sense and Feeling of Which, the Soul skippeth in its Body for great Joy, and in the Strength of this Virgin Love exulteth, and praiseth the Great God for His blessed Gift of Grace.

I will set down here a short Description how it is when the Bride thus embraceth the Bridegroom, for the Consideration of the Reader, who perhaps hath not yet been in this Wedding-Chamber. It may be that he will be desirous to follow us, and to enter into the Inner Choir, where the Soul joineth Hands and danceth with Sophia, or the Divine Wisdom.

I.

When that which is mentioned above cometh to pass, the Soul rejoiceth in its Body, and saith,

PRAISE, Thanksgiving, Strength, Honor, and Glory, be to Thee, O great God, in Thy Power and Sweetness, for that Thou hast redeemed me from the Anguish of the fiery Driver. O Thou Fair Love! My heart embraceth Thee; where hast Thou been so long? I thought I was in Hell in the Anger of God. O Gracious Love! Abide with me, I beseech Thee, and be my Joy and Comfort. Lead me in the right WAY. I give myself up into Thy Love. I am dark before Thee, do Thou enlighten me. O Noble Love, give me Thy Sweet Pearl; put it I pray Thee into me.

O Great God in Christ Jesus, I praise and magnify Thee now in Thy Truth, in Thy Great Power and Glory, for that Thou hast forgiven me my Sins, and filled me with Thy Strength. I shout for Joy before Thee in my new Life, and extol Thee in Thy Firmament of Heaven, which none can open but Thy Spirit in Thy Mercy. My Bones rejoice in Thy Strength, and my Heart delighteth itself in Thy Love. Thanks be to Thee forever, for that

Thou has delivered me out of Hell, and turned Death into Life in me. O Sweet Love! Let me not depart from Thee again. Grant me Thy Garland of Pearl, and abide in me. O be my own proper Possession, that I may rejoice in Thee forever.

Upon this, the Virgin Sophia saith to the Soul,

MY nobel Bridegroom, my Strength and Power, thou art a thousand Times welcome. Why hast thou forgotten Me so long, that I have been constrained in great Grief to stand without the Door and knock? Have I not always called thee and entreated thee? But thou hast turned away thy Countenance from Me, and thine Ears have declined My Entreaties. Thou couldst not see My Light, for thou didst walk in the Valley of Darkness. I was very near thee, and entreated thee continually, but thy Sinfulness held thee Captive in Death, so that thou knewest Me not. I came to thee in great Humility, and called thee, but thou wert rich in the Power of the Anger of God, and didst not regard My Humility and Lowliness. Thou hast taken the Devil to be thy Paramour, who hath defiled thee thus, and built up his Fort of Prey in thee, and turned thee quite away from My Love and Faith into his hypocritical Kingdom of Falsehood; wherein thou hast committed much Sin and Wickedness, and torn thy Will off from My Love. Thou hast broken the Bond of Wedlock, and set thy Love and Affection upon a Stranger, and suffered Me thy Bride, whom God did give thee, to stand alone in the extinguished Substance, without the Power of thy fiery Strength. I could not be joyful without thy fiery Strength, for thou art My Husband; My shining Brightness is made manifest by thee. Thou canst manifest My hidden Wonders in thy fiery Life, and bring them into Majesty; and yet without Me thou art but a dark House, wherein is nothing but Anguish, Misery, and horrible Torment.

O noble Bridegroom, stand still with thy Countenance towards Me, and give Me thy Rays of Fire. Bring thy Desire into Me, and enkindle Me thereby, and then I will bring the Rays of My Love, from My Meekness into thy fiery Essence, and be united with thee forever.

O My Bridegroom, how well am I, now that I am in Union with thee! O kiss Me with thy Desire in thy Strength and Power, and then I will show thee all My Beauty, and will rejoice and solace Myself with thy sweet Love and shining Brightness in thy fiery Life. All the Holy Angels rejoice with us, to see us united again. My dear Love, I now entreat thee to stay faithful to Me, and do not turn thy Face away from Me any more. Work thou thy Wonders in My Love, for which Purpose God hath created thee and brought thee into Being.

II.

The Soul saith again to its Noble Sophia , its Love, that is born again in it,

O my Noble Pearl, and opened Flame of Light in my anxious fiery Life, how Thou changest me into Thy Joy! O Beautiful Love, I have broken my Faith with Thee in my Father Adam, and with my fiery Strength have turned myself to the Pleasure and Vanity of the outward World. I have fallen in Love with a Stranger, and would have been constrained to walk in the Valley of Darkness in this strange Love, if Thou hadst not come into the House of my Misery, in Thy great Faithfulness, by Thy piercing through and destroying God's Anger, Hell, and dark Death, and restoring Thy Meekness and Love to my fiery Life.

O Sweet Love! Thou hast brought the Water of Eternal Life out of the Fountain of God, with Thee into me, and refreshed me in my great Thirst. I behold in Thee the Mercy of God, which was hidden from me before by the strange Love. In Thee I can rejoice; Thou changest my Anguish of Fire into great Joy in me. O amiable Love, give me Thy Pearl, that I may continue in this Joy forever.

Upon this the Noble Sophia answereth the Soul again, and saith,

MY dear Love and faithful Treasure, thou highly rejoicest Me in thy Beginning. I have indeed broken into thee through the deep Gates of God, through God's Anger, through Hell and

Death, into the House of thy Misery, and have graciously bestowed My Love upon thee, and delivered thee from the Chains and Bonds wherewith thou wert fast bound. I have kept My Faith with thee, even though thou hast not kept thine with Me. But now thou desireth an exceeding great Thing of Me, which I cannot willingly trust in thy Hands. Thou wouldest have My Pearl as thy proper own. Remember, I pray, O My beloved Bridegroom, that thou didst carelessly lose it before in Adam; and thou thyself standest yet in great Danger, and walkest in two dangerous Kingdoms; for in thy original Fire thou walkest in that Country wherein God calleth Himself a strong jealous God, and a consuming Fire. The other Kingdom which thou walkest in, is the outward World, wherein thou dwellest in the vain corrupt Flesh and Blood, and where the Pleasures of the World and Assaults of the Devil beset thee every Hour. Thou mayest perhaps in thy great Joy bring Earthliness again into My Beauty, and thereby darken My Pearl; or thou mayest possibly grow proud, as Lucifer did, when he had the Pearl in his Possession, and so turn thyself away from the Harmony of God, as he did, and then I must be deprived of My Love forever afterwards.

No. I will keep My Pearl in Myself, and dwell in the Heaven in thee, in thy extinguished, but now in Me, revived, Humanity, and reserve My Pearl for Paradise, until thou puttest away this Earthliness from thee, and then I will give it to thee to possess. But I will readily present to thee My pleasant Countenance, and the sweet Rays of the Pearl, during the Time of this Earthly Life. I will dwell with the Pearl Itself in the inner Choir, and be thy faithful loving Bride. I cannot espouse Myself with thy earthly Flesh, for I am a heavenly Queen, and My Kingdom is not of this World. Yet I will not cast thy outward Life away, but refresh it often with My Rays of Love; for thy outward Humanity shall return again. But I cannot admit to My Embraces the Beast of Vanity, neither did God create It in Adam with a Purpose to have It so gross and earthly. But in Adam thy Desire, through the Power of its strong Lust, formed this beastial Grossness, from and with all the Essences of the awakened Vanity of the earthly

Property, wherein Heat and Cold, Pain and Enmity, Division and Corruption subsist.

Now, My dear Love and Bridegroom, do but yield thyself up into My Will; I will not forsake thee in this earthly Life in thy Danger. Though the Anger of God should pass upon thee, so that thou shouldst grow affrighted and disheartened, or shouldst think that I had deserted thee, yet I will be with thee and preserve thee, for thou thyself knowest not what thine Office is. Thou must work and bear Fruit in this Life's Time. Thou art the Root of this Pearl-Tree; Branches must be produced out of thee, which must all be brought forth in Anguish. But I come forth together with thy Branches in their Sap, and produce Fruit upon thy Boughs, and thou knowest it not; for the Most High hath ordered, that I should dwell with and in thee.

Wrap thyself up therefore in Patience, and take Heed of the Pleasure of the Flesh. Break the Will and Desire thereof; bridle it as an unruly Horse; and then I will often visit thee in the fiery Essence, and give thee My Kiss of Love. I will bring a Garland for thee out of Paradise with Me, as a Token of My Affection, and put it upon thee, and thou shalt rejoice in it. But I give thee not My Pearl for a Possession during this Life's Time. Thou must continue in Resignation, and hearken what the Lord playeth on His Instrument in thy Harmony in thee. Moreover, thou must give Sound and Essence to thy Tune, out of My Strength and Virtue, for thou art now a Messenger of His Word, and must set forth His Praise and Glory. For this Cause it is that I have contracted Myself a-new with thee, and set My triumphal Garland upon thee; which I have gotten in the Battle against the Devil and Death. But the Crown of Pearl wherewith I crowned thee, I have laid aside for thee. Thou must wear that no more till thou art become pure in My Sight.

III.

The Soul saith further to the Noble Sophia,

O Thou Fair and Sweet Consort, what shall I say before Thee? Let me be wholly committed unto Thee; I cannot preserve myself. If Thou wilt not give me Thy Pearl, I submit to Thy Will; but give me Thy Rays of Love, and carry me safely through my Pilgrimage. Do Thou awaken and bring forth what Thou wilt in me; I will from henceforth be Thy own. I will or desire nothing for myself, but what Thou Thyself wilt through me. I had fooled away Thy Sweet Love, and broken my Faith with Thee, whereby I was fallen into the Anger of God. But seeing that of Love Thou didst come to me into the Anguish of Hell, and hast delivered me from Torment, and received me again for Thy Consort, I will now therefore break my Will for Thy Love's Sake, and be obedient unto Thee, and wait for Thy Love. I am satisfied now that I know Thou art with me in all my Troubles, and wilt not forsake me.

O Gracious Love, I turn my fiery Countenance to Thee. O fair Crown, take me quickly into Thee, and bring me forth from Unquietness. I will be Thine forever, and never depart from Thee more.

The Noble Sophia answereth the Soul very comfortably, and saith,

MY noble Bridegroom, be of good Comfort. I have betrothed thee to Me in My highest Love, and contracted Myself with thee in My Faithfulness. I will be with thee and in thee always to the End of the World. I will come to thee and make My Abode with thee, in thy inner Chamber. Thou shalt drink of My Fountain; for now I am thine, and thou art Mine; the Enemy shall not separate Us. Work thou in thy fiery Property, and I will put My Rays of Love into thy Working. And so We will plant and manure the Vineyard of Jesus Christ. Afford thou the Essence of Fire, and I will afford the Essence of Light, and the Increase. Be thou the Fire, and I will be the Water, and thus We will perform that in this World for which God hath appointed Us, and serve Him in His Temple, which We ourselves are. Amen.

To The READER

BELOVED Reader, count not this an uncertain Fiction; it is the true Ground, Sum and Substance of all the Holy Scriptures. For the Book of the Life of Jesus Christ is plainly set forth therein, as the Author of a Certainty knoweth; it being the WAY that he himself hath gone. He giveth thee the best Jewel that he hath. God grant His Blessing with it. A heavy Sentence and Judgement are gone forth against the Mocker of this. Be thou therefore warned, that thou mayest avoid the Danger, and obtain the Benefit.

A MORNING PRAYER

Commending ourselves to God when we rise, before we suffer any other Thing to enter into us.

BLESS me, O God, the Father, Son, and Holy Ghost, Thou only True God. I thank Thee through Jesus Christ our Lord and Saviour, for the Preservation of me, and for all other Benefits. I now commend myself, both Soul and Body, and all that Thou hast set me to do in my Employment and Calling, into Thy Protection. Be Thou the Beginning of my Conceptions, my Undertakings, and all my Doings. Work Thou so in me, that I may begin all Things to the Glory of Thy Name, and accomplish them in Thy Love for the Good and Service of my Neighbor. Send Thy holy Angel along with me, to turn the Temptations of the Devil and corrupt Nature away from me. Preserve me from the Malice of evil Men; make all my Enemies reconcilable to me, and bring my Mind into Thy Vineyard, that I may labor in my Office and Employment, and behave as Thy obedient Servant therein. Bless me, and all that I am to go about and do this Day, with the Blessing of Thy Love and Mercy. Continue Thy Grace and Love in Jesus Christ upon me, and give me a Mind cheerfully to follow Thy Leading and execute Thine Appointment. Let Thy Holy Spirit guide me in my Beginning, and my Progress, on to my Last End, and be the Willing, Working, and Accomplishing of all in me. Amen.

AN EVENING PRAYER

When we have finished our daily Employment, and are going to Rest

I LIFT my Heart to Thee, O God, Thou Fountain of Eternal Life, and give Thee Thanks through Jesus Christ, Thy Beloved Son, our Lord and Saviour, for having protected and preserved me this Day from all Mischief that might have befallen me. I commend to Thy Disposal my Condition and Employment, together with the Work of my Hands, and humbly repose them on Thee. So fill my Soul with Thy Spirit, that neither the grand Enemy, the Devil, nor any other evil Influence or Desire, may find Harbour therein. Let my Mind only delight in Thee in Thy Temple, and let Thy good Angel stay with me, that I may rest safely in Thy Power, and under Thy Protection. Amen.

Rev. 21, 6-7: I am Alpha and Omega, the Beginning and the End. I will give unto him that is athirst of the Fountain of the Water of Life freely. He that overcometh shall inherit all Things, and I will be his God, and he shall be My Son.

Of True Resignation

OR

Dying to SELF

by
Jacob Boehme 1575-1624,
The Teutonic Theosopher

SHOWING

How Man must DAILY die to his OWN Will in SELF; how he must bring his Desire into God, and what he should ask and desire of God.
LIKEWISE

How he must spring up out of the dying sinful Man, with a new Mind and Will through the Spirit of Christ.
ALSO

What the Old and New Man are, and what each of them is in Life, Will and Practice.

Composed by a Soul that loveth all
who are Children of JESUS CHRIST, under the Cross.

Brought forth in the 1600's by a humble shoemaker; translated into English over 100 years later; suppressed and hidden away until recently in theological archives around the world... a worthy personal study not just for academics but for all those who are spiritually grounded in the WORD, who are learning to hear the Lord, and who hunger for more.

Christ saith, If any Man will come after Me, let him DENY HIMSELF, and take up his Cross daily, and follow Me.
-- Matthew 16,24; Mark 8,34; Luke 9,23.

Peter saith to Christ, Behold, we have forsaken All, and followed Thee.
                    -- Matthew 19,27; Mark 10,28; Luke 18,28.

THE FIRST CHAPTER

We have a clear Example in Lucifer, and also in Adam the first Man, of what SELF doeth, when it getteth the Light of Nature to be its OWN, and when it can walk with the Understanding in its OWN Dominion. We see also in Men learned in Arts and Sciences, that when they get the Light of this outward World or Nature into the Possession of their Reason, nothing cometh of it but Pride of themSELVES. And yet all the World so vehemently desireth and seeketh after this Light as the best Treasure; and indeed it is the best Treasure this World affordeth, if it be rightly used.

2. But while SELF, viz. Reason, is captivated and fast bound in a close and strong Prison, that is to say, in the Anger of God, and in Earthliness, it is very dangerous for a Man to make Use of the Light of Knowledge in SELF, as if it were in the Possession of SELF.

3. For the Wrath of the Eternal and Temporary Nature will soon take Pleasure in it, and then SELF and a Man's own Reason, will rise up in Pride, and depart from the true resigned Humility towards God, and will no longer eat of the Fruit of Paradise, but instead eat of the Property of SELF, viz. of that Dominion of Life, wherein Good and Evil are mixed as Lucifer and Adam did. Who both entered with the Desire of SELF back again into the Original, out of which the Creatures were brought forth and entered into the Condition of the Creatures; Lucifer into the Center and wrathful Nature, into the Matrix or Womb which bringeth forth Fire, and Adam into the earthly Nature, into the Matrix of the outward World, viz. into the Lust after Good and Evil.

4. This happened to them both, because they had the Light of Understanding shining in SELF, in which they could behold themselves, whereby the Spirit of SELF went into the Imagination, (viz. into a Desire to get to the Center,) that they might exalt themselves in Might, Power, and Knowledge. Now when Lucifer sought after the Mother of Fire in his Center, and thought to

reign therewith over the Love of God and all the Angels, and when Adam also desired to try in the Essence what the Mother or Root was from whence Evil and Good did spring, and purposely brought his Desire thereinto, in order to thereby become knowing and full of Understanding thereby: Both Lucifer and Adam were captivated in their evil or false Desire in the Mother, and broke off themselves from Resignation which proceeds from God, and so were caught by the Spirit of the Will, by the Desire in the Mother. Which Desire immediately got the Dominion in Nature; and so Lucifer stuck fast in the wrathful Source of Fire, and that Fire became manifest in the Spirit of his Will, whereby the Creature in its Desire became an Enemy to the Love and Meekness of God.

5. Adam in like Manner, was immediately caught by the earthly Mother, which is Evil and Good, created out of the Anger and Love of God, and compacted into one Substance. Whereupon the earthly Property instantly got the Dominion in Adam, and from thence Heat and Cold, Envy and Anger, and all Malice and Contrariety to God became manifest, and bore Rule in him.

6. But if they had not brought the Light of Knowledge into SELF, then the Glass of the Knowledge of the Center and of the Original of the Creature, viz. of the Power which it had in itself would not have been manifested, from whence the Imagination and Lust did arise.

7. As also we often see at this Day how the same Error bringeth Danger upon the enlightened Children of God; in whom when the Sun of the great Presence of God's Holiness shineth, by which the Life passeth into Triumph, and then Reason beholds itself therein as in a Glass, and the Will goeth on in SELF, in its OWN searching, and will try what the Center is out of which the Light shineth, and will of its OWN Motion and Strength force itSELF into it, how that from thence arise abominable Pride and SELF-Love; so that its (the Creature's) own Reason, which is but a Mirror or Glass of the Eternal Wisdom, supposeth itSELF to be greater than it is; and then whatsoever it doeth, it thinketh

God's Will doeth in and by it, and that he is a Prophet; though it is moved only by itSELF, and goeth on in its OWN Desire, in which the Center of Nature presently riseth up, and entereth into that false Desire of SELF against God, and so the Will entereth into SELF-Conceit and Exaltation.

8. Then the subtle Devil insinuateth himself into the Creature, and sifteth the Center of Nature, and bringeth evil or false Desires into it, so that a Man becometh as it were drunken in SELF, and still persuades himself that he is driven by God, by which Means the good Beginning, wherein the Divine Light shone in Nature, cometh to be spoiled, and so the Light of God departeth from him.

9. Yet the outward Light of the outward Nature still remaineith shining in the Creature; for its own SELF throweth itself thereinto, and supposeth that it is still the first Light of God; but it is not so. And into this SELF-Exaltation in the Light of its outward Reason, the Devil throweth himself again, (though in the first Light, which was Divine, he had been forced to depart) now returning with the seven-fold Desire, of which Christ spake, saying, When the unclean Spirit departeth out of a Man, he wandereth through dry Places seeking Rest, and findeth none; and then he taketh to himself seven Spirits worse than himself, and returneth to his first House; and finding it swept and garnished, he dwelleth therein, and so it is worse with that Man than it was before.

10. This House, that is thus swept and garnished, is the Light of Reason in SELF. For if a Man bringeth his Desire and Will into God, and then goeth on in Abstinence from this wicked Life, and heartily desireth the Love of God, then that Love will indeed manifest itself to him with its most friendly and cheerful Countenance, by which the outward Light also is kindled. For where the Light of God is kindled, there all will be Light; the Devil cannot stay there, but must depart thence; and then he searcheth through the Mother of the Original of Life, viz. the Center, but finds that it is become a dry feeble Place. For the Anger of God, viz, the Center of Nature, is in its own Property

altogether feeble, barren and dry and cannot get the Dominion in its own wrathful Principle. Satan continually searcheth through these Places to find an open Gate to enter with his Desire, and so to sift the Soul that it might come to exalt its SELF.

11. And now if the Spirit of the Will of the Creature throweth itself with the Light of Reason back into the Center, viz. into SELF, and entereth into SELF-Exaltation, then it goeth forth again from the Light of God, and presently the Devil findeth an open Gate for him to enter in at, and a garnished House to dwell in, viz. the Light of Reason. Then he taketh to himself the seven Forms of the Property of Life in SELF, viz. the Flatterers which are departed from God into SELF; and there he entereth and putteth his Desire into the Lust of SELF and evil Imaginations, wherein the Spirit of the Will beholdeth itself in the Forms of the Properties of Life in the outward Light, and then the Man sinketh into himself as if he were drunk, and the Stars lay hold on him, and bring their strong Influences into him, (into outward Reason) that he might seek the Wonders of God there, that so they may manifest themselves therein. For all Creatures groan and long after God. And though the Stars cannot apprehend the Spirit of God, yet they would rather have a House of Light wherein they may rejoice, than a House shut up, wherein they can have no Rest.

12. Thus such a Man goeth on as if he were drunk, in the Light of the outward Reason, which is called the Stars, and apprehendeth great and wonderful Things, and hath a continual Guide, therein. And then the Devil presently watcheth to see if any Gate standeth open for him, through which he may kindle the Centre of Life, that so the Spirit of the Will may mount aloft in Pride, Self-Conceit, or Covetousness; (from whence Self-Arrogancy ariseth, the Will of Reason desiring to be honored;) for it supposeth it hath attained the Sum of all Happiness, when it hath gotten the Light of Reason, and can judge the House of hidden Mysteries that is shut up; which nevertheless God can easily unlock. The deluded Man thereupon supposeth that now he hath reached the Mark, and that Honour is due to him,

because he hath gotten the Understanding of Reason, and never considereth that the Devil maketh himself merry with his Desire in his seven Forms of Life of the Center of Nature, nor what abominable Error he setteth up.

13. From this Understanding of Reason false Babel is brought forth in the Christian Church on Earth, wherein Men rule and teach by the Conclusions of Reason, and have set the Child which is drunk in its own Pride and SELF-Desire, as a fair Virgin upon the Throne.

14. But the Devil is entered into its seven Forms of Life of the Center, viz. into its own SELF-conceited Reason, and continually bringeth his Desire into this trimmed and decorated Virgin, which the Stars receive. He is her Beast on which she rideth, well adorned with her own Powers of Life, as may be seen in the Revelation of St. John. Thus hath this Child of SELF taken into its Possession the outward Glance of Divine Holiness, viz. the Light of Reason, and supposeth itSELF to be the fair Child in the House, though the Devil hath his Lodging within it all the while.

15. And thus it is with all those who have been once enlightened by God, and afterwards go forth again from true Resignation, and wean themselves from the pure Milk of their Mother, viz. true Humility.

THE SECOND CHAPTER

Here Reason will object and say, Is it not right for a Man to attain the Light of God, and also the Light of the outward Nature and Reason, that he may be able to order his Life wisely, as the Scripture directeth?

2. Yes, it is very right; nothing can be more profitable to a Man, neither is he capable of any Thing better; nay, it is a Treasure above all Earthly Treasures for a Man to have the Light of God and of Time, for it is the Eye of Time and of Eternity.

3. But mark how thou oughtest to use it; when the Light of God first manifesteth itself in the Soul, it shineth forth as Light from a Candle, and kindleth the outward Light of Reason immediately; yet it yieldeth not itself wholly up to Reason, so as to be under the Dominion of the outward Man. No, the outward Man beholdeth himself in this through-shining Lustre, as he doth his Likeness in a Looking-Glass, whereby he presently learneth to know himself, which is good and profitable to him.

4. Now, when he doth so, Reason, which is the creaturely SELF, cannot do better than to behold itself in the SELF of the Creature, and not enter with the Will of the Desire into the Center in seeking itself. If it doth, it breaketh itself off from the Substance of God, (which riseth together with the Light of God, of which the Soul ought to eat, and refresh itself therewith,) and eateth of the outward Substance and Light, and thereby draweth the Venom into itself again.

5. The Will of the Creature ought to sink wholly into itself with all its Reason and Desire, accounting itself an unworthy Child that is no whit worthy of this so high a Grace; nor should it arrogate any Knowledge or Understanding to itself, or desire of God to have any Understanding in its creaturely SELF; but sincerely and simply sink down into the Grace and Love of God in Christ Jesus, and desire to be as it were dead to itSELF and its own Reason, in the Divine Life, and wholly resign itself to the Spirit of God in Love, that He may do how and what He will with it as with His own Instrument.

6. Its own Reason ought not enter upon any Speculation as to the Ground of Divine or human Matters; nor to will and desire any Thing but the Grace of God in Christ. And as a Child continually longeth after the Breasts of the Mother, so must its Hunger be continually entering into the Love of God, and not suffer itself to be broken off from that Hunger by any Means. When the outward Reason or SELF riseth up and triumpheth in the Light, saying, I have the true Child, then the Will of the Desire must bow itSELF down to the Earth, and bring itself into the deepest Humility and most simple Ignorance, and say, Thou art foolish, and hast nothing but the Grace of God. Thou must wrap thySELF up in that Belief with great Humility, and become nothing at all in thySELF, and neither know nor love thy SELF. All that thou hast, or is in thee, must esteem itSELF as nothing but a mere Instrument of God; and thou must bring thy Desire only into God's Mercy, and go forth from all thy OWN Knowing and Willing; and esteem it as nothing at all, nor ever entertain any Will to enter into it again.

7. As soon as this is done the natural Will becometh weak and faint, and then the Devil is not able to sift it thus any more with his evil Desire, for the Places of his Rest become very powerless, barren and dry; and then the Holy Spirit proceeding from God, taketh Possession of the Forms of Life, and maketh His Dominion to prevail. He kindleth the Forms of Life with His Flames of Love, and then the high Knowledge of the Center of all Things ariseth, according to the inward and outward Constellation or Complexion of the Creature, in a very subtle drying Fire, attended with great Delight. Whereupon the humbled Soul presently desires to sink down into that Light, and esteems itself to be nothing and quite unworthy of It.

8. And thus its own Desire pierceth into that nothing, viz.(into that wherein God createth) and doth what God wills therein, and the Spirit of God springeth forth through the Desire of the resigned Humility, and so the human Self immediately followeth the Spirit of God in Trembling and humble Joy; and

thus it may behold what is in Time and Eternity, for All is present before it.

9. When the Spirit of God riseth up as a Fire and Flame of Love, then the Sprit of the Soul descendeth, and saith, Lord, Glory be to Thy Name, not to me; Thou art able to take to Thyself Virtue, Power, Strength, Wisdom, and Knowledge; do as Thou wilt; I can do nothing; I know nothing; I will go no whither but whither Thou leadest me as Thy Instrument; do Thou in me and with me what Thou wilt.

10. In such a humble and total Resignation the Spark of Divine Power falleth into the Center of the Forms of Life, as a Spark into Tinder, and kindleth it, viz. the Fire of the Soul, which Adam had made to be a dark Coal in himself, so that it glimmereth. And when the Light of Divine Power hath kindled itself therein, the Creature must go on as an Instrument of God's Spirit, and speak what the Spirit of God dictateth to it; and then it is no more in its own proper Possession, but is the Instrument of God.

11. But the Will of the Soul must without ceasing, in this fiery driving, sink into nothing, viz. into the deepest Humility in the Sight of God. For no sooner doth the Will of the Soul in the least Measure go on in its OWN Speculation or Searching, but Lucifer layeth hold of it in the Center of the Forms of Life, and sifteth it so that it entereth into SELF. It must therefore continue close to resigned Humility, as a Well doth to its Spring, and must suck and drink of God's Fountain, and not depart from the Ways of God at all.

12. For as soon as the Soul eateth of SELF, and of the Light of outward Reason, it goeth on in its OWN Opinion; and then its Doings, which it sets forth for Divine, are but from the outward Constellation, or Influence of the Stars, which presently layeth hold on the Soul, and maketh it dry. And then the Soul goeth on in Errors, till it yield itSELF up again into Resignation, and acknowledging itSELF anew to be a defiled Child, resisteth Reason and so getteth the Love of God again. Which is harder to

do in that Case than it was at first; for the Devil bringeth in strong Doubts now, and will not easily leave his Fort of Prey.

13. This may be seen clearly in the Saints of God from the Beginning of the World. For many who have been driven by the Spirit of God, have yet oftentimes departed from Resignation into SELF, viz. into their OWN Reason and Will, in which Satan hath cast them into Sins, and into the Anger of God; as appeareth by David and Solomon, also by the Patriarchs, Prophets, and Apostles; who have oftentimes committed great Errors when they have departed from Resignation into SELF, viz. into their own Reason and Lust.

14. Therefore, it is necessary for the Children of God to know how to behave themselves when they will learn the WAY of God. They must beat down and cast away their very Thoughts; and desire nothing, nor have the least Will to learn any Thing, unless they find themselves to be in true Resignation; so that God's Spirit leadeth, teacheth, and guideth Man's Spirit, and that the human Will which is attached to itSELF, be wholly broken off from its OWN Lust, and resigned to God.

15. All Speculation in the Wonders of God is very dangerous, for the Spirit of the Will may soon be captivated therewith, unless the Spirit of the Will goeth or walketh after the Spirit of God, and then it hath Power in the resigned Humility to behold the Wonders of God.

16. I do not say that a Man should search and learn nothing in natural Arts and Sciences. No; such Knowledge is useful to him; but a Man must not begin with his OWN Reason. Man ought not only to govern his Life by the Light of outward Reason, which is good in itself; but should sink with that Light into the deepest Humility before God, and set the Spirit and Will of God foremost in all his searching, so that the Light of Reason may see and know Things through the Light of God. And though Reason may be very wise in its own Sphere, and help a Man to much Knowledge, yet it must not arrogate such Wisdom and Knowledge to itSELF, as if they were in its OWN Possession,

but give the Glory thereof to God, to Whom alone all Wisdom and Knowledge belongeth.

17. For the more deeply Reason sinketh itSELF down into simple Humility in the Sight of God, and the more unworthy it accounts itSELF in His Sight; the more truely it dieth from SELF-desire and the more thoroughly the Spirit of God penetrateth it, and bringeth it into the highest Knowledge, so that at length it may come to behold the great Mysteries and Wonders of God. For the Spirit of God worketh only in resigned Humility, in that which neither seeketh nor desireth itSELF. The Spirit of God taketh hold of whatsoever desireth to be simple and lowly before Him, and bringeth it into His Wonders. He hath Pleasure only in those that fear and bow themSELVES before Him.

18. For God hath not created us for ourSELVES only, but to be Instruments of His Wonders, by which He desireth to manifest His Wonders. The resigned Will trusteth God, and expecteth all Good from Him alone; but SELF-Will ruleth itself, for it is broken off from God. All that SELF-Will doeth is Sin and is against God; for it is gone out of that Order wherein He created it, into Disobedience, and desireth to be its OWN Lord and Master.

19. When a Man's OWN Will dieth from itSELF, then it is free from Sin, for it desireth nothing but that which God desireth of His Creature; it desireth only to do that for which God hath created it and that which God will do by it; and though it is and must be involved in the Doing, yet it is but the Instrument of the Doing, by which God doth what He will.

20. For this is the true Faith in Man, viz. to die from himSELF; that is, from his OWN Desire; and in all his Undertakings and Designs to bring his Desire into the Will of God, and arrogate the doing of nothing to himSELF, but esteem himSELF in all his Doings to be a Servant or Minister of God, and to think that all he doeth, and undertaketh, is for God. For in such a Disposition the Spirit of God leadeth him into true Uprightness and Faithfullness towards his Neighbor. For he thinketh thus within himself, I do my Work not for myself, but

for God, Who hath called and appointed me to do it; I am but a Servant in His Vineyard. He listeneth continually after the Voice of his Master, Who within him commandeth him what he shall do. The Lord speaketh in him, and biddeth him do what He would have to be done by him.

21. But SELF doeth what outward Reason from the Stars commandeth, into which Reason the Devil flyeth with his Desire. All whatever SELF doth is without the Will of God, and is done altogether in the Fantasy, that the Anger of God may accomplish its Pastime therewith.

22. No Work done without the Will of God can reach the Kingdom of God; it is all but an unprofitable Imagery, or SELF-wrought work, in this great Agitation of Mankind. For nothing is pleasing to God, but what He Himself doth by the resigned Will, as His Instrument. For there is but one only God in the Essence of all Essences, and all that which worketh with Him in that Essence, is one Spirit with Him; but that which worketh in itSELF only, in its OWN Will, is in itSELF only, and not in His Dominion. It is indeed under that universal Dominion of Nature, whereby He holdeth subject to Him every Life, evil and good, but not under that special Divine Government in Himself, which comprehendeth the Good only. Nothing is Divine which walketh and worketh not in the Will of God.

23. Christ saith, Every Plant which my heavenly Father hath not planted, shall be rooted out and burned in the Fire. All the works of Man, which he hath wrought without the Will of God, shall be burnt up in the last Fire and given to the Wrath of God, viz. to the Pit of Darkness to recreate itself withal. For Christ saith, He that is not with Me is against Me; and he that gathereth not with Me scattereth. Whosoever worketh, and doeth it not in a resigned Will with Confidence in God, doeth but make desolate and scatter; it is not acceptable to God. For nothing is pleasing to Him but that which He willeth with His Spirit, and doeth by His own Instrument.

24. Therefore, whatsoever is done by the Conclusions of human SELF in Matters of Religion, is a mere Fiction. It is Babel,

and but a Work of the Stars, and of the outward World, and not acknowledged by God to be His Work. It is only the Play of the wrestling Wheel of Nature, wherein Good and Evil wrestle one with the other; what the one buildeth, the other destroyeth. And this is the great Misery of the vain Turmoiling of Men, the Issue whereof must be left to the Judgement of God.

25. Whosoever therefore stirreth or laboreth much in such Turmoilings, worketh but for the Judgement of God; for no whit of it is perfect and permanent. It must all be separated in the Putrefaction. For that which is wrought in the Anger of God will be received thereby, and kept in the Mystery of its Desire to the Day of God's Judgement, when Evil and Good shall be severed.

26. But if a Man turn and go forth from himSELF, and enter into the Will of God, then also that Good which hath been wrought in and by him, shall be freed from the Evil which he hath wrought. As Isaiah saith, Though your Sins be as red as Scarlet, yet if ye turn and repent, they shall become as Wool, yea, as white as Snow. For the Evil shall be swallowed up in the Wrath of God into Death, and the Good shall spring forth as a Sprout out of the wild Earth.

THE THIRD CHAPTER

Whosoever therefore intendeth to do any good and perfect Work, wherein he hopeth eternally to rejoice, let him depart from himSELF, viz. from his OWN Desire, and enter into Resignation, into the Will of God, and work with God. And then though the earthly Desire of SELF in Flesh and Blood cleaveth to him, yet if the Will of the Soul doth not receive that Desire into it, SELF cannot perform any Work. For the resigned Will continually destroyeth the Substance of SELF again, so that the Anger of God cannot reach it. And if it should happen to reach it sometimes, as may be the Case, yet the resigned Will prevaileth with its superior Power, and then it beareth the Figure of a victorious Work in the Wonders, and may inherit the Filiation [or Childship]. Therefore it is not good to speak or do any Thing, when Reason is kindled in and by the Desire of SELF because that Desire springeth from, and worketh in, the Anger of God; by which a Man would suffer Loss. For his Work is brought into that Anger, and kept there to the great Day of God's Judgement.

2. Every evil or false Desire, whereby a Man deviseth how to gather to himSELF by Craft much worldly Gain from his Neighbor to his Neighbor's Hurt, is taken into the Anger of God, and belongeth to the Judgement. Wherein all Things shall be made manifest and every Power and Essence, every Cause and Effect, both in Good and Evil, shall be presented to every one in the Mystery of the Revelation.

3. All evil Works, done purposely, belong to the Judgement of God. But he that turneth from the SELF Will, goeth out from the Power of them, and those his Works belong to the Fire. All Things shall and must be made manifest in the End. For therefore God brought His working Power into Essence or Substance, that His Love and Anger might be made manifest, and become a Representation of His Deeds of Wonder, to His Glory.

4. And every Creature ought to know that it should continue in that Condition wherein it was created; otherwise it runneth on in Contrariety and Enmity to the Will of God, and bringeth itself

into Pain. For every intelligent Creature that hath lost its Place or State wherein God first created it, is in Disorder and Misery, till it recovereth the same. A Creature which is created out of Darkness hath no Pain in the Darkness; as a venomous Serpent hath no Pain from its Venom. The Venom is its Life; but if it should lose its Venom, and have some good Thing instead brought into it, and be made manifest in its Essence, that would be Pain and Death to it. Thus Good is Torment to a Being whose nature is evil, and Evil is in like Manner Pain and Death to the Good.

5. Man was created of, for, and in Paradise; of, for and in the Love of God; but if he brings himself into Anger, which is as a poisonous Pain and Death, then that contrary Paradisical Life of Love is a Pain and Torment to him.

6. If the Devil had been created out of the wrathful Matrix, for and in Hell, and had not had the Divine Ens or Essence, he could have no Pain in Hell. But he, being created for and in Heaven, and yet having stirred up the Source or Property of Darkness in himself, and thereby brought himself totally into Darkness, therefore the Light is now a Pain to him; that is, it causeth an everlasting Despair of God's Grace, and a continual Enmity to God; because God cannot endure him in Himself, but hath cast him out. Therefore, the Devil is angry and wrathful against his own Mother, of whose Essence and Substance he hath his Original, viz. the Eternal Nature, which keepeth him Prisoner in his own Place, as a Revolter or fallen Spirit, and sporteth in him with its Property of Anger. And, seeing he would not bear his Part in promoting the Divine Joy, in and for which he was created, therefore he must now do the contrary, and be an Enemy to all Goodness. For, of God, and in Him, are all Things, Darkness and Light, Anger and Love, Fire and Light; but He calleth Himself God, only as to the Light of His Love.

7. There is an eternal Contrariety between Darkness and Light, neither of them comprehendeth the other, and neither of them is the other; and yet there is only one Essence, Being, or Substance, wherein they both subsist. But there is a Difference in

the Quality and Will; yet the Essence or Substance is not divided, but a Principle maketh the Division. So that the one is a nothing in the other, and yet it is there, but not manifest in the Property of that Thing wherein it is.

8. For the Devil continued in his own Dominion or Principality, not indeed in that wherein God created him, but in the aching painful Birth of Eternity, in the Center of Nature and Property of Wrath, in the Property which begetteth Darkness, Anguish and Pain. Indeed he is a Prince in the Place of this World, but in the first Principle, in the Kingdom of Darkness, in the Pit or Abyss.

9. Not in the Kingdom of the Sun, Stars, and Elements; he is no Lord or Prince there, but only in the wrathful Part, viz. in the Root of the Evil of every Thing; and yet he hath not Power to do what he pleaseth with that.

10. For there is some Good in every Thing, which holdeth the Evil captive and shut up in the Thing; but he can walk and rule only in the evil Part or Property when it stirreth up an evil Desire in itSELF, and bringeth its Desire into Wickedness. This indeed the inanimate Creature cannot do; but Man can do it through the inanimate Creature, if he brings the Center of his Will, with the Desire out of the Eternal Center into it, which is the Ground of Enchantment and false Magic. The Will of the Devil can also enter into that Evil whereinto Man bringeth the Desire of his Soul, which is born also out of the Eternal Nature.

11. For the Original of the Soul and of Angels, out of the Eternal Nature is the same. But the Devil hath no further Power over the Time, or temporary Condition of this World, than in the great Turba or Turba Magna, the Curse; wheresoever that kindleth itself in the eternal and temporal Wrath, there he is busy, as in Wars, Fighting, and Strife, as also in great Tempests without Water. In fire he proceeds as far as the Turba (Mischief or Hurt) goeth in great Showers or Tempests of Thunder, Lightning, and Hail; but he cannot direct them, for he is not Lord or Master in them, but Servant only.

12. Thus the Creature stirreth up with its own Desire, Good and Evil, Life and Death. The human Angelical Desire standeth in the Center of the eternal Nature which is without Beginning; and wherever it kindleth itself, whether in Good or Evil, it accomplisheth its Work in that.

13. Now God created every Thing for and in that wherein it should be; the Angels for and in Heaven, and Man for and in Paradise. If therefore the Desire of the Creature goeth forth from its own Mother, then it entereth into the contrary Will and into Enmity, and it is tormented with the Contrariety therein, and so a false Will ariseth in a good; and then the good Will entereth into its nothing again, viz. into the End of Nature and Creature, and so leaveth the Creature in its OWN Evil or Wickedness, as appeareth by Lucifer and also Adam; and had not the Will of the Love of God met with Adam, and of mere Mercy entered into the Humanity or human Nature again, there could be no good Will in Man.

14. Therefore all Speculation and Inquiry about God's Will is a vain Thing, unless the Mind be converted. For when the Mind standeth captivated in the SELF-Desire of the earthly Life, it cannot comprehend what the Will of God is; it runneth on but in SELF, from one Way into another, and yet findeth no Rest; for SELF-Desire evermore bringeth Disquiet. But when it sinketh itself wholly into the Mercy of God, desiring to die from itSELF, and to have God's Will for a Guide to the Understanding, so that it acknowledgeth and esteemeth itSELF as nothing, and willeth nothing but what God willeth, then shall it both know and do the Will of God. And if the Desire of Anger in the earthly Flesh should go along or join with the Devil's Imagination, and assault the Will of the Soul, yet the resigned Desire cryeth to God and saith, Abba, loving Father, deliver me from Evil. And then, though the earthly Will should grow too strong in the Wrath of God by the Infection of the Devil, the Desire of Anger would work but in or upon itself. According to what St. Paul saith, Now, if I sin, I do it not, but Sin that dwelleth in my Flesh: Also, Now I serve the Law of God in my Mind, but in my Flesh the Law of

Sin. Paul meaneth not that the Will of the Mind or Soul should consent to the Will of the Flesh; but Sin is so strong in the Flesh, viz. the awakened Anger of God in SELF, that oftentimes the Mind is brought into Lust, as it were by Force, through the evil Incitements of the wicked, or else by beholding worldly Pomp and Glory; so that it absolutely beareth down the resigned Will, and ruleth by Force.

15. Now when Sin is wrought in the Flesh, then the Wrath sporteth itself therewith, and catcheth at the resigned Will; and then the resigned Will cryeth to God for Deliverance from the Evil, and prayeth that God would remove the Guilt away from it, and bring Sin into the Centre, viz. into Death, that it might die.

16. And St. Paul saith further, Now, there is no Condemnation to those who are in Christ Jesus, who are called according to the Purpose of God; that is, those who in that Purpose of God in which He first called Man, are again called in the same Calling, to stand again in that Purpose of God, wherein he originally created Man to be His Image and Likeness.

17. So long as Man's OWN Will standeth in SELF, so long it is not in the Purpose and Calling of God; it is not called, for it is gone forth from its original right Place; but when the Mind turneth itself back again into the Calling, viz. into Resignation, then the Will is in the Calling of God, that is, in the Place for and in which God created it, and then it hath Power to become the Child of God again; as it is written, He hath given us Power to become the Children of God.

18. The Power which He hath given us is His Purpose, for and in which He created Man in His Image. This God hath brought again into the human Nature, and hath given Power unto that Power to break the Head of Sin in the Flesh, namely, the Will and Desire of the Serpent; that is, the resigned Will in Christ treadeth upon the Head of the Desire of the sinful Will of the Serpent, and killeth again the Sins which were committed. This Power that is given becometh a Death to Death, and the Power of Life to Life.

19. Therefore no Man can make any Excuse, as if he could not will. Indeed, while he sticketh fast in himSELF, in his OWN Desire, and serveth only the Law of Sin in the Flesh, he cannot. For he is kept back, as being a Servant of Sin; but when he turneth the Center of his Mind away, and directeth it into the Will and Obedience of God, then he can.

20. Now the Center of the Mind is come out of Eternity, out of God's Omnipotence; it can bring itself into what it will, and whither it will. For that which is out of the Eternal, hath no Law. But the Will hath a Law to obey God, and is born out of the Mind, and must not rend or tear itself away from that out of which God created it.

21. Now God created the Will of the Mind for and in Paradise, to be a Companion, with Him in the Kingdom of Divine Joy. It ought not to have removed itself from thence; but since it hath removed itself from thence, God hath brought His Will again into the Flesh, and in His new-brought-in Will, hath given us Power to bring our Wills into it, and to kindle a new Light therein, and so to become His Children again.

22. God hardeneth no Man; but Man's OWN Will, which goeth on in the fleshly Life of Sin, hardeneth his OWN Heart. The Will of SELF bringeth the Vanity of this World into the Mind, which is thereby shut up, and continueth so.

23. God, so far as He is called God, and is God, cannot will any Evil; for there is but one only Will in God, and that is Eternal Love, a Desire of that which is His Like, viz. Power, Beauty, and Virtue.

24. God desireth nothing but what is like His own Desire: His Desire receiveth nothing but what Itself is.

25. God receiveth no Sinner into His Power and Virtue, unless the Sinner go forth from His Sins, and enter with the Desire into God. And then, He will not cast out those that so come unto Him. He hath given to the Will an open Gate in Christ, saying, "come unto Me all ye that are heavy laden with Sins, and I will refresh you; take My Yoke upon you, that is, the Cross of the Enmity in the Flesh. This was the Yoke of Christ,

which He had to bear for the Sins of all Men. This Cross or Yoke the resigned Will must also take upon itself in the evil earthly sinful Flesh, and bear it after Christ in Patience and Hope of Deliverance. It must also continually break the Head of the Serpent, in and through Christ's Will and Spirit, and kill and destroy the earthly Will in God's Anger, not letting it rest on the soft Bed when Sin is committed, and thinking to repent one Time or other.

26. No, no, the earthly Will groweth strong, fat, and wanton upon this soft Bed, but as soon as the Light of God shineth in thee, and sheweth Sin to thee, the Will of thy Soul must sink itself down into the Passion and Death of Christ, and wrap itself up close therein. It must take the Passion of Christ into its Possession, and be a Lord over the Death of Sin by the Death of Christ, and kill and destroy it in the Death of Christ.

27. The Will of Sin [thy outward SELF] must die, though it be never so unwilling. Be at Enmity therefore with the voluptuous earthly Flesh; give it not what it would have; let it fast and suffer Hunger till its tickling ceases. Account the Will of the Flesh thine Enemy, and do not do what the Desire in the Flesh willeth, and then thou shalt bring a Death upon the deathful Property in the Flesh.

28. Regard not any Scorn of the World, as considering that it doth but scorn thine Enemy, and that is become a Fool to it. Nay, do thou thyself account it thy Fool, which Adam caused thee to possess, and made to be thy false Heir. Cast out of the House the Son of the Bond-Woman, that strange Child which God did not give to be in the House of Life in Adam at the Beginning; for the Son of the Bond-Woman must not inherit with the Son of the Free-Woman.

29. The earthly Will is but the Son of the Bond-Woman. For the Four Elements should have been Man's Servants, but Adam hath brought them into the Sonship, or adopted them into himself. Therefore God said to Abraham, when He had opened the Covenant of the Promise in him, Cast out the Son of the Bond-Woman, for he shall not inherit with the Son of the Free.

This Son of the Free is Christ, which God of His Grace hath brought again into the Flesh for us, namely, a new or renewed Mind, wherein the Will, viz. the Eternal Will of the Soul, may draw and drink the Water of Life, of which Christ speaketh, saying, Whosoever shall drink of this Water that I will give him, It shall spring up in him, and be a Fountain of Eternal Life. This Fountain is the Renovation of the Mind or Will of the Soul.

30. Therefore I say that all Fictions and Devices to come to God by, let them have what Name soever they will, which Men contrive and invent for Ways to God, are but lost Labor and vain Endeavours, without a new Mind. There is no other Way to God, but a new Mind, which turneth from Wickedness, and entereth into Repentance for the Sins it hath committed. Which goeth forth from its Iniquity and willeth it no more; but wrappeth its Will up in the Death of Christ, and with all Earnestness dieth from the Sin of the Soul in the Death of Christ, so that it willeth Sin no more.

31. And though all the Devils should press hard upon it, and enter with their Desire into the fleshly Mind, yet the Will of the Soul must stand still and hide itself in the Death of Christ, willing and desiring nothing but the Mercy of God.

32. No hypocritical Flattery, or outward comforting ourselves availeth at all; as when Men will cover Sin and Iniquity in the Flesh with the Satisfaction of Christ, while they remain in SELF still. Christ saith, Except ye turn and become as Children, ye shall not see the Kingdom of God. The Mind must become as wholly new, as in a Child that knoweth nothing of Sin. Christ saith also, Ye must be born anew, or else, ye shall not see the Kingdom of God. There must arise a Will wholly new in the Death of Christ. It must be brought forth out of Christ's Incarnation or Entering into the Humanity, and rise in Christ's Resurrection.

33. Now before this can be done, the Will of the Soul [SELF] must die in the Death of Christ; for in Adam it received the Son of the Bond-Woman, viz. Sin into it. This the Will must cast out, and the poor captive Soul must wrap itself up in the

Death of Christ earnestly with all the Power it hath, so that the Son of the Bond-Woman, viz. the Sin that is in it may die in the Death of Christ.

34. In very deed Sin must die in the Will of the Soul, or else there can be no Vision of God. For the earthly Will, in Sin and the wrathful Nature, shall not see God. It is only the regenerated Nature, the new inward Man, that is capable of the Divine Vision or Enjoyment. The Soul must put on the Spirit and Flesh of Christ; it cannot inherit the Kingdom of God in this earthly Tabernacle. For the Kingdom of Sin hangeth to it outwardly, which must putrify in the Earth, and rise again in new Power.

35. Hypocrisy, Flattery, and verbal Forgiveness, avail nothing. We must be Children, not by outward Imputation, but by being born of God from within, in the new inward Man, which is resigned in and to God.

36. All such Flattery of ourselves by saying, Christ hath paid the Ransom, and made satisfaction for Sin, and that He died for our Sins, is a false and vain Comfort, if we also do not die from Sin in Him, and put on His Merit in new Obedience, and live therein.

37. He that is a bitter Enemy and Hater of Sin, can and may comfort himself with the Sufferings of Christ. He that doth not willingly see, hear, or taste Sin, but is at Enmity with it, and would willingly always do that which is well and right, if he knew but what he ought to do; such a one hath indeed put on the Sprirt and Will of Christ, and is His true Disciple.

38. But the outward Flattery of being accounted a Child of God by Imputation or external Application, is false and vain. The Work done in, or by, the outward Flesh only, doth not make the Child of God; but the working of Christ in the Spirit maketh, and indeed is, the Child of God. Which inward Working is so powerful that it shineth forth as a new Light in the outward Life; and proveth itself to be the Child of God by its external Conduct and Actions.

39. For if the Eye of the Soul be Light, then the whole Body is Light in all its Members. Now if any Man boast himself to be a

Child of God, and yet suffereth his Body to burn in Sins, he is no true Child, nor capable of the Inheritance; but lieth bound by the Chains of the Devil in gross Darkness. And if he doth not find in himself an earnest and sincere Desire of Well-doing in Love, then his Pretence to the Childship is but an Invention of Reason proceeding from SELF. He cannot see God, unless he be born a-new, and show forth by his Power and Life, that he is His true Child. For there is no Fire but hath Light in it; and if the Divine Fire be in the Mind, it will shine forth, and the Mind will do that which God will have to be done.

40. But perhaps thou wilt say, I have a Will indeed to do so; I would willingly do it, but I am so hindered that I cannot.

41. Nay, thou vile Man, God draweth thee to be His Child, but thou wilt not; the soft Cushion in Evil is dearer to thee than to be so readily parted with. Thou preferrest the Joy of Wickedness to the Joy of God. Thou art wholly swallowed up in SELF still, and livest according to the Law of Sin, and that is what hindereth thee. Thou art unwilling to die from the Pleasure of the Flesh, and therefore thou art not in the Filiation (Sonship). God draweth thee to it, but thou thySELF wilt not yield.

42. O how fine a Thing would Adam think it, if he might be taken into Heaven with this Will of the voluptuous Flesh about him, and have the Child of Wickedness, that is full of Deceit, set upon the Throne of God. Lucifer also would fain have had it so, but he was spewed out.

43. It is a troublesome Thing to mortify the evil Will of SELF; none are willing to do it. We would all gladly be the Children of God, if we might be so with this rough Garment of fallen Nature about us. But that cannot be. This World passeth away, and the outward Life must die; what Good can the Adoption in the mortal Body of Flesh and Blood only do me?

44. If we would inherit the Filiation, we must also put on the new Man which alone can inherit it, as being like the Deity. God will have no Sinners in Heaven, but only such as have been born a-new and become Children, and to have put on Heaven.

45. Therefore it is not so easy a Matter to become a Child of God, as Men imagine. Indeed, it is not a troublesome Thing to him that hath put on the Filiation, whose Light shineth; for it is Joy to such a one. But to turn the Mind and destroy SELF, there is a strong and continued Earnestness requisite, and such a stout and steady Purpose, that if the Body and Soul should part asunder by it, yet the Will would persevere constantly, and not enter again into SELF.

46. A Man must wrestle till the dark Center that is shut up tight, breaketh open, and the Spark lying hid therein kindleth and from thence the noble Lily-Branch sprouteth, as from the divine Grain of Mustard-Seed as Christ saith. A Man must pray earnestly, with great Humility, and for a while become a Fool in his own Reason, and see himself void of Understanding therein, until Christ be formed in this new Incarnation.

47. And then when Christ is born, Herod is ready to kill the Child, which he seeketh to do outwardly by Persecutions, and inwardly by Temptations, to try whether this Lily-Branch will be strong enough to destroy the Kingdom of the Devil, which is manifested in the Flesh.

48. Then this Destroyer of the Serpent is brought into the Wilderness, after he is baptized with the Holy Spirit, and tempted and tried whether or not he will continue in Resignation to the Will of God. In which Temptation he must stand so fast, that if Need require, he would leave all earthly Things, and even the outward Life, to be a Child of God.

49. No temporal Honor must be preferred before Filiation. But he must with his Will leave and forsake it all, and not account it his OWN, but esteem himself as a Servant only in it, who is to obey his Master. He must leave all worldly Propriety. We do not mean that he may not have or possess any Thing; but his Heart must forsake it, and not bring his Will into it, nor count it his OWN. For if he setteth his Heart upon it, he hath no Power to serve them that stand in Need with it.

50. SELF is but a Slave to its temporal Possessions, but Resignation ruleth over all that it hath. SELF must do what the

Devil will have it do in fleshly Voluptuousness and Pride of Life; but Resignation treadth it all under with the Feet of the Mind. SELF despiseth that which is lowly and simple; but Resignation sitteth down with the lowly in the Dust. It saith, I will be simple in myself, and understand nothing, lest my Understanding should exalt itself and sin. I will lie down in the Courts of my God at His Feet, that I may serve my Lord in that which He commandeth me. I will know nothing of myself, that the Will and Power of my Lord may lead and guide me, and that I may only do what God doth through me, and will have done by me. I will sleep in myself until the Lord awaken me with His Spirit; and if He will not, then will I look up to Him in Silence, and wait for His Commands.

51. Beloved Brethren: Men at this Time boast much of Faith; but where is it to be found? The modern Faith is but the History. Where is that Child which believeth that Jesus has been born within his own soul? If that Child were in Being, and did believe that Jesus is born, it would also draw near to the sweet Child Jesus, and receive Him and nurse Him.

52. Alas! the Faith of this Day is but historical, a mere Assent to the matter of Fact that Jesus Christ was born, lived and died; that the Jews killed Him; that He left this World, and is not King on Earth in the outward Man; and the Faith of this Day allows that Men may do what they please, and need not die from Sin and their evil Lusts. All this the wicked Child SELF rejoiceth in, that it may fatten the Devil by living deliciously.

53. This showeth plainly that true Faith was never weaker since Christ's Time, than it is now. When nevertheless the World cryeth aloud, and saith, We have got the true Faith; and contend about a Child, with a Contention which has never been worse since Men have been on Earth.

54. If thou art truly Zion, and hast that new born Child which was lost and is found again, then let It be seen in Power and Virtue. Let us all openly see the sweet Child Jesus brought forth by thee, and that thou art His Nurse. If not, then the true

Children in Christ will say, thou hast found nothing but the Cradle of the Child, that is, the History.

55. Where hast thou the sweet Child Jesus, thou that art so exalted with the History, and with thy false and seeming Faith? O how will the Child Jesus visit thee one Day in the Father's Property, the Property of Anger, in thy own Turba which thou hast fatted! It calleth thee now in Love, but thou wilt not hear, for thine Ears are stopped with Covetousness and Voluptuousness. Therefore the Sound of the Trumpet shall one Day alarm thee with the hard Thunder-clap of thy Turba, and rouse thee up, if perhaps thou wilt then seek and find the sweet Child Jesus.

56. Beloved Brethren, this is a Time of Seeking, of Seeking and Finding. It is a Time of Earnestness; whom it toucheth, it toucheth Home. He that watcheth shall hear and see it; but he that sleepeth in Sin, and saith in the fat Days of his Belly, All is peace and quiet; we hear no Sound from the Lord, shall be blind. But the Voice of the Lord hath sounded in all the Ends of the Earth, and a Smoke riseth, and in the Midst of the Smoke there is a great Brightness and Splendor. Hallelujah. Amen.

Shout unto the Lord in Zion, for all Mountains and Hills are full of His Glory. He flourisheth like a green Branch, and who shall hinder It. Hallelujah.

OF Regeneration, OR THE New Birth

SHEWING

How he that earnestly seeketh Salvation, must suffer himself to be brought out of the confused and contentious Babel, by the Spirit of CHRIST, that he may be born a-new in the Spirit of CHRIST, and live to Him only.

by Jacob Boehme
1575-1624,
The Teutonic Theosopher

Come out of Babylon, my People, that ye be not Partakers of her Sins, and that ye receive not of her Plagues; for her Sins have reached unto Heaven, and God hath remembered her Iniquity.

-- Rev. xviii. 4:

Brought forth in the 1600 s by a humble shoemaker; translated into English over 100 years later; suppressed and hidden away until recently in theological archives around the world... a worthy personal study not just for academics but for all those who are spiritually grounded in the WORD, who are learning to hear the Lord, and who hunger for more.

THE AUTHOR'S PREFACE TO THE READER.

Though I have in my other Writings, set down a clear description of Regeneration, or the New-Birth, from the Ground thereof; yet because everyone hath them not, neither hath everyone the Capacity to understand them; I have therefore, as a Service to the simple Children of Christ, here set down a short Sum concerning the New-Birth.

But if any desire to search the deep Ground from whence all floweth, and have the Gift to understand it, let them read

I. The Three Principles of the Divine Essence.

II. The Threefold Life of Man.

III. The Forty Questions of the Original Essence, Substance, Nature, and Property of the Soul.

IV. The Incarnation and Birth of Jesus Christ the Son of God; also of his Suffering, Death, and Resurrection.

V. The Six Points treating of the Three Worlds how they are in one another as one; and yet make Three Principles, viz., Three Births or Centers.

VI. The Mysterium Magnum, which is an Interpretation upon Genesis.

And in them he shall find all that he can ask, and that as deep as the Mind of Man is able to reach. I have written this for the true Israelites, that is, for the Hungry and Thirsty Hearts that long after the Fountain of Christ, who are my Fellow Members in the Spirit of Christ: But not for the Ishmaelites and Scorners, for they have a Book within them, wherewith they vex, persecute, and suppress the Children of Christ that are under the Cross; and yet, though it be unwillingly and unwittingly to themselves, they must be Servants to such Children of Christ.

THE FIRST CHAPTER.

Showing how Man should consider himself.

CHRIST said, Except ye turn and become as Children, ye shall not see the kingdom of God. Again, he said to Nicodemus; Except a Man be born again, of Water and of the Spirit, he cannot enter into the Kingdom of God; for that which is born of the Flesh is Flesh, and that which is born of the Spirit is Spirit.

2. Also the Scripture positively declareth, that the fleshly natural Man receiveth not the Things of the Spirit of God, for they are Foolishness unto him, neither can he know or conceive them.

3. Now seeing that all of us have Flesh and Blood and are mortal, as we find by Experience, and yet the Scripture saith, that We are the Temples of the Holy Ghost, who dwelleth in us, and that the Kingdom of God is within us, and that Christ must be formed in us; also, that He will give us his Flesh for Food, and his Blood for Drink: And that, Whosoever shall not eat of the Flesh of the Son of Man, and drink his Blood hath no Life in him. Therefore we should seriously consider, what kind of Man in us it is, that is capable of being thus like the Deity.

4. For it cannot be said of the mortal Flesh that turneth to Earth again, and liveth in the Vanity of this World, and continually lusteth against God; that it is the Temple of the Holy Ghost; much less can it be said that the New Birth cometh to pass in this earthly Flesh, which dieth and putrifieth, and is a continual House of Sin.

5. Yet seeing that it remaineth certain, that a True Christian is born of Christ, and that the New Birth is the Temple of the Holy Ghost which dwelleth in us, and that the New Man only, that is born of Christ, partaketh of the Flesh and Blood of Christ; it appeareth that is is not so easy a Matter to be a Christian.

6. And that Christianity doth not consist in the mere knowing of the History, and applying the Knowledge thereof to ourselves, saying that Christ died for us, and hath destroyed

Death and turned it into Life in us, and that He hath paid the Ransom for us, so that we need do nothing but comfort ourselves therewith, and steadfastly believe that it is so.

7. For we find of ourselves that Sin is living, lusting, strong, and powerfully working in the Flesh, and therefore it must be somewhat else, which doth not co-operate with Sin in the Flesh, nor willeth it, that is the New-Birth in Christ.

8. For St. Paul saith, There is no Condemnation to them that are in Christ Jesus. And further, Should we that are Christians be yet Sinners? God forbid, seeing we are dead to Sin in Christ.

9. Besides, the Man of Sin cannot be the Temple of the Holy Ghost; and yet, there is no Man that sinneth not, for God hath shut up all under Sin. As the Scripture saith, No one living is righteous in thy Sight, if thou imputest his Sins to him. The righteous Man falleth seven Times a Day; and yet it cannot be meant that the righteous falleth and sinneth, but his mortal and sinful Man. For the righteousness of a Christian in Christ cannot Sin.

10. Moreover, St. Paul saith, Our Conversation is in Heaven, from whence we expect our Saviour Jesus Christ. Now, if our Conversation be in Heaven, then Heaven must be in us; Christ dwelleth in Heaven; and then if we are his Temple, that Temple Heaven must be in us.

11. But for all this, seeing Sin tempteth us within us, whereby the Devil hath within us an Access to us, therefore Hell also must be in us too, for the Devil dwelleth in Hell; wheresoever he is, he is in Hell. and cannot come out of it. Yea, when he possesseth a Man, he dwelleth in Hell, viz., in the Anger of God in that Man.

12. Therefore we ought to consider well what Man is, and how he is a Man; and then we shall find that a true Christian is not a mere historical new Man, as if it were enough for us outwardly to confess Christ, and believe that he is the Son of God, and hath paid the Ransom for us. For Righteousness availeth nothing, imputed from without, that is, by believing only that it is

so imputed. But it is an inherent Righteousness born in us, by which we become the Children of God, that availeth.

13. And as the earthly Flesh must die, so also the Life and Will must die from Sin, and be as a Child that knoweth nothing, but longeth only after the Mother which brought it forth. So likewise must the Will of a Christian enter again into its Mother, viz., into the Spirit of Christ, and become a Child in itself, in its own Will and Power, having its Will and Desire inclined and directed only towards its Mother. And a new Will and Obedience in Righteousness, which willeth Sin no more, must rise from Death out of the Spirit of Christ in him.

14. For that Will is not born a-new, which desireth and admitteth Vanity into itself; and yet there remaineth a Will which longeth after Vanity, and sinneth, even in the new-born or regenerate Man. Therefore the Image or Nature of Man should be well understood, and how the New-birth cometh to pass; seeing it is not wrought in the mortal Flesh, and yet is wrought truly and really in us, in Flesh and Blood, in Water and Spirit, as the Scripture saith.

15. We should therefore rightly understand what Kind of Man it is in us, that is the Member of Christ, and Temple of God who dwelleth in Heaven. And then also what Kind of Man it is, that the Devil ruleth and driveth; for he cannot meddle with the Temple of Christ, nor doth he care much for the mortal Flesh; and yet there are not three Men in one another, for all make but one Man.

16. Now if we will understand this rightly, we must consider Time and Eternity, and how they are in one another; also Light and Darkness, Good and Evil; but especially the Original of Man.

This may be thus apprehended.

17. THE outward World with the Stars and four Elements, wherein Man and all Creatures live, neither is, nor is called God. Indeed God dwelleth in it, but the Substance of the outward World comprehendedeth him not.

18. We see also that the Light shineth in Darkness, and the Darkness comprehendeth not the Light, and yet they both dwell

in one another. The four Elements are also an Example of this; which in their Original are but one Element, which is neither hot nor cold, nor dry, nor moist; and yet by its stirring separateth itself into Four Properties, viz., into Fire, Air, Water, and Earth.

19. Who would believe that Fire produceth or genereateth Water? And that the Original of Fire could be in Water, if we did not see it with our Eyes in Tempests of Thunder, Lightening, and Rain; and did not find also, that in living Creatures, the essential Fire of the Body dwelleth in the Blood, and that the Blood is the Mother of the Fire, and the Fire is the Father of the Blood.

20. And as God dwelleth in the World, and filleth all Things, and yet possesseth nothing; and as the Fire dwelleth in Water, and yet possesseth it not: Also, as the Light dwelleth in Darkness, and yet possesseth not the Darkness; as the Day is in the Night, and the Night in the Day, Time in Eternity, and Eternity in Time; so is Man created according to the outward Humanity; he is the Time, and in the Time, and the Time is the outward World, and it is also the outward Man.

21. The inward Man is Eternity and the Spiritual Time and World, which also consisteth of Light and Darkness, viz., of the Love of God, as to the eternal Light, and of the Anger of God as to the eternal Darkness; whichsoever of these is manifest in him, his Spirit dwelleth in that, be it Darkness or Light.

22. For Light and Darkness are both in him, but each of them dwelleth in itself, and neither of them possesseth the other; but if one of them entereth into the other, and will possess it, then that other loseth its Right and Power.

23. The passive loseth its Power; for if the Light be made manifest in the Darkness, then the Darkness loseth its Darkness, and is not known or discerned. Also on the contrary, if the Darkness arise in the Light and get the upper-hand, then the Light and the Power thereof are extinguished. This is to be observed also in Man.

24. The Eternal Darkness of the Soul is Hell, viz., an aching Source of Anguish, which is called the Anger of God; but the

Eternal Light in the Soul is the Kingdom of Heaven, where the fiery Anguish of Darkness is changed into Joy.

25. For the same Nature of Anguish, which in the Darkness is a Cause of Sadness, is in the Light a Cause of the outward and stirring Joy. For the Source or Original in Light, and the Source in Darkness are but one Eternal Source, and one Nature, and yet they, viz., the Light and Darkness, have a mighty Difference in the Source; the one dwelleth in the other and begetteth the other, and yet is not the other. The Fire is painful and consuming, but the Light is yielding, friendly, powerful, and delightful, a sweet and amiable Joy.

26. This may be found also in Man; he is and liveth in three Worlds; the First is the Eternal dark World, viz., the Centre of the Eternal Nature, which produceth or generateth the Fire, viz., the Source or Property of Anguish.

27. The Second is the Eternal light World, which begetteth the Eternal Joy, which is the Divine Habitation wherein the Spirit of God dwelleth, and wherein the Spirit of Christ receiveth the human Substance, and subdueth the Darkness, so that it must be a Cause of Joy in the Spirit of Christ in the Light.

28. The Third is the outward visible World in the four Elements and the visible Stars; though indeed every Element hath its peculiar Constellation in itself, whence the Desire and Property arise, and is like a Mind.

29. Thus you may understand, that the Fire in the Light is a Fire of Love, a Desire of Meekness and Delightfulness; but the Fire in the Darkness is a Fire of Anguish, and is painful, irksome, inimicitious and full of Contrariety in its Essence. The Fire of the Light hath a good Relish or Taste, but the Taste in the Essence of Darkness is unpleasant, loathsome and irksome. For all the Forms or Properties in the Eternal Nature, till they reach to Fire, are in great Anguish.

THE SECOND CHAPTER.

How Man is created.

HERE we are to consider the Creation of Man. Moses saith, God created Man in His Image, in the Image of God created he him. This we understand to be both out of the eternal and temporal Birth; out of the inward and spiritual World, which he breathed into him, into the created Image; and then out of the Substance of the inward spiritual World, which is holy.

31. For as there is a Nature and Substance in the outward World; so also in the inward spiritual World there is a Nature and Substance which is spiritual; from which the outward World is breathed forth, and produced out of Light and Darkness, and created to have a Beginning and Time.

32. And out of the Substance of the inward and outward World Man was created; out of, and in the Likeness of the Birth of all Substances. The Body is a Limbus (an Extract or a kind of Seed, which containeth all that which the Thing from whence it is taken hath) of the Earth, and also a Limbus of the heavenly Substance; for the Earth is breathed forth out-spoken, or created out of the dark and light World. In the Word Fiat (or creating Word) viz., in the eternal Desire Man was taken out of the Earth, and so created an Image out of Time and Eternity.

33. This Image was in the inward and spiritual Element, from whence the four Elements proceed and are produced. In that one Element was Paradise; for the Properties of Nature from the Fire-dark-and-light-World were all in Harmony and Agreement in Number, Weight, and Measure. One of them was not manifested more eminently than another, therefore was there no Frailty therein. For no one Property was predominant over another, neither was there any Strife or Contrariety among the Powers and Properties.

34. Into this created Image God breathed the Spirit and Breath of Understanding out of the three Worlds, as one only Soul which, as to its Original Principle or Essence, is, or

consisteth in, the inward dark Fire-World of the eternal spiritual Nature; according to which God calleth himself a strong jealous God, and a consuming Fire.

35. And this now is the eternal creaturely great Soul, a magical Breath of Fire, in which Fire consisteth the Original of Life, from the great Power of Separation. God's Anger, or the eternal Darkness, is in this Property, so far as Fire reacheth without giving Light.

36. The second Property of the Breath of God is the Spirit of the Source of Light, proceeding from the great fiery Desire of Love, from the great Meekness; according to which God calleth himself a loving, merciful God; in which consisteth the true Spirit of Understanding, and of Life in Power.

37. For as Light shineth from Power, and as the Power of Understanding is discerned in the Light, so the Breath of the Light was joined to the Breath of the Fire of God, and breathed into the Image of Man.

38. The third Property of the Breath of God was the outward Air with its Constellation or Astrum, wherein the Life and Constellation of the outward Substance and Body did consist. This he breathed into his Nostrils; and as Time and Eternity hang together, and as Time is produced out of Eternity, so the inward Breath of God hung to the outward.

39. This three-fold Soul was at once breathed into Man; and each Substance of the Body received the Spirit according to its Property. The outward Flesh received the outward Air and its Constellations, for a rational and vegetative Life, to the Manifestation of the Wonders of God; and the Light Body or Heavenly Substance received the Breath of the Light of the great Divine Powers and Virtues; which Breath is called the Holy Ghost.

40. Thus the Light pierced through the Darkness, viz., through the dark Breath of Fire, and also through the Breath of the outward Air and its Constellation or Astrum, and so deprived all the Properties of their Power, that neither the Anguish of the Breath of Fire in the inward Property of the Soul, nor Heat nor

Cold, nor any of all the Properties of the outward Constellation, might or could be manifested.

41. The Properties of all the three Worlds in Soul and Body were in equal Agreement, Temperature, and Weight. That which was inward and holy ruled through and over the outward, that is, the outward Parts of the outward Life, of the outward Stars and Constellations and the Four Elements; and that original and universal Power of the inward over the outward constituted the Holy Paradise.

42. And thus Man was both in Heaven and also in the outward World, and was Lord over all the Creatures of this World. Nothing could destroy him.

43. For such was the Earth also, until the Curse of God broke forth. The Holy Property of the Spiritual World sprung up through the Earth, and brought forth Holy Paradisaical Fruits, which Man could then eat in a magical Paradisaical Manner.

44. And had neither need of Teeth, nor Entrails in his Body. For as the Light swalloweth up Darkness, and as the Fire devoureth Water, and yet is not filled therewith, just such a Centre Man also had for his Mouth to eat withal, according to the Manner of Eternity.

45. And he could also generate his Like out of himself, without any dividing or opening of his Body and Spirit, in such a Manner as God generated the outward World; who did not divide himself; but did in his Desire, viz., in the Word Fiat, manifest himself, and brought that same Desire into a Figure according to the Eternal Spiritual Birth. So also Man was created an Image and Likeness of God in that Respect, according to Time and Eternity, out of both Time and Eternity, yet in and for an immortal Life, which was without Enmity or Contrariety.

46. But the Devil having himself been a Prince and Hierarch in the Place of this World, and cast out for his Pride into the dark, anguishing, painful and hostile Property and Source, into the Wrath of God, envied Man the Glory of being created in and for the Spiritual World, the Place which he himself once possessed; and therefore brought his Imagination or Desire into

the Image of Man, and made it so lusting, that the dark World, and also the outward World arose in Man, and departed from the equal Agreement and Temperature wherein they stood, and so one predominated over the other.

47. And then the Properties were each of them separately made manifest in itself, and each of them lusted after that which was like itself. That which was out of the Birth of the dark World, and also that which was out of the Birth of the light World, would each of them eat of the Limbus of the Earth, according to its Hunger; and so Evil and Good became manifest in Adam.

48. And when the Hunger of the Properties went into the Earth, from whence the Properties of the Body were extracted, then the Fiat drew such a Branch out of the Earth, as the Properties could eat of in their awakened Vanity; for this was possible.

49. For the Spirit of the strong and great magical Power of Time and Eternity was in Adam, from which the Earth with its Properties was breathed forth; and so the Fiat, viz., the strong Desire of the eternal Nature, attracted the Essence of the Earth. And thus God let the Tree of Knowledge of Good and Evil grow for Adam, according to his awakened Properties; for the great Power of the Soul and of the Body caused it.

50. And then Man must be tried, whether he would stand and subsist in his own Powers, before the Tempter the Devil, and before the Wrath of the eternal Nature; and whether the Soul would continue in the equal Agreement of the Properties in true Resignation under God s Spirit, as an Instrument of God s Harmony, a tuned Instrument of divine Joyfulness for the Spirit of God to strike upon. This was tried by that Tree, and this severe Commandment was added, Thou shalt not eat thereof, for on that Day that thou eatest thereof, thou shalt surely die.

51. But it being known to God that Man would not stand, and that he had already imagined and lusted after Good and Evil, God said, It is not good for Man to be alone, we will make him an Help-meet for him.

52. For God saw that Adam could not then generate magically, having entered with his Lust into Vanity. Now therefore Moses saith, God caused a deep Sleep to fall upon him, and he slept; that is, seeing Man would not continue in the Obedience of the Divine Harmony in the Properties, submitting himself to stand still as an Instrument of the Spirit of God; therefore God suffered him to fall from the Divine Harmony into an Harmony of his own, viz., into the awakened Properties of Evil and Good; the Spirit of his Soul went into these.

53. And there in this Sleep he died from the Angelical World, and fell under the Power of the outward Fiat, and thus bade farewell to the Eternal Image which was of God s begetting. Here his Angelical Form and Power fell into a Swoon and lay on the Ground.

54. And then by the Fiat God made the Woman out of him, out of the Matrix of Venus, viz., out of that Property wherein Adam had the Begettress in himself; and so out of one Body he made two, and divided the Properties of the Tinctures, viz., the watery and fiery Constellations in the Element; yet not wholly in Substance but in the Spirit, viz., the Properties of the watery and fiery Soul.

55. And yet it is but one Thing still, only the Property of the Tincture was divided; the Desire of Self-Love was taken out of Adam, and formed into a Woman according to his Likeness. And thence it is that Man now so eagerly desireth the Matrix of the Woman, and the Woman desireth the Limbus of the Man, viz., the Fire-Element, the Original of the true Soul, by which is meant the Tincture of Fire; for these two were one in Adam, and therein consisted the Magical Begetting.

56. And as soon as Eve was made out of Adam in his Sleep, both Adam and Eve were at that Instant set and constituted in the outward natural Life, having the Members given them for Propagation, after the manner of the Brute Animals, and also the fleshly Carcase, into which they might put their gross Earthliness, and live like Beasts.

57. Of which the poor Soul that is captivated in Vanity is at this Day ashamed; and sorry that its Body hath gotten such a beastial monstrous Shape. Nothing can be clearer than this. For it is because Mankind are ashamed of their Members and Nakedness, that they borrow their Clothing from the earthly Creatures. For this they would not have done, had they not lost the Angelical Form, and assumed that of a Beast.

58. This borrowed Clothing, together with the awakened Earthliness, and Subjection to the Powers of Heat and Cold, is a plain and full Proof to Man, that he is not truly at Home in this World. For all earthly Appetites, Cares, and Fears, together with this false Clothing, must perish and be severed from the Soul again.

59. Now when Adam awoke from Sleep, he beheld his Wife, and knew that she came out of him; for he had not yet eaten of Vanity with his outward Mouth, but with the Imagination, Desire, and Lust only.

60. And it was the first Desire of Eve, that she might eat of the Tree of Vanity, of Evil and Good, to which the Devil in the Form of a Serpent persuaded her, saying, That her Eyes should be opened, and she should be as God himself; which was both a Lie and a Truth.

61. But He told her not, that she should lose the Divine Light and Power thereby: He only said, her Eyes should be opened, that she might taste, prove, and know Evil and Good, as he had done. Neither did he tell her that Heat and Cold would awake in her, and that the Property of the outward Constellations would have great Power over the Flesh and over the Mind.

62. His only Aim was that the Angelical Image, viz., the Substance which came from the inward Spiritual World, might disappear in them. For then they would be constrained to live in Subjection to the gross Earthliness, and the Constellations or Stars; and then he knew well enough that when the outward World perished, the Soul would be with him in Darkness. For he saw that the Body must die, which he perceived by that which God had intimated; and so he expected still to be Lord to all

Eternity in the Place of this World, in his false Shape which he had gotten; and therefore he seduced Man.

63. For when Adam and Eve were eating the Fruit, Evil, and Good, into the Body, then the Imagination of the Body received Vanity in the Fruit, and then Vanity awaked in the Flesh, and the dark World got the Upperhand and Dominion in the Vanity of the Earthliness; upon which the fair Image of Heaven, that proceeded out of the Heavenly Divine World, instantly disappeared.

64. Here Adam and Eve died to the Kingdom of Heaven, and awaked to the outward World, and then the fair Soul as it stood in the Love of God, disappeared as to the holy Power, Virtue, and Property; and instead thereof, the wrathful Anger, viz., the dark Fire World, awoke in it, and so the Soul became in one Part, viz., in the inward Nature, a half Devil, and in the outward Part as related to the outward World, a Beast.

65. Here are the Bounds of Death and the Gates of Hell, for which Cause God became Man, that he might destroy Death, defeat the Devil s Purpose, and change Hell into great Love again.

66. Let this be told you, Ye Children of Men; it is told you in the Sound of a Trumpet, that you should instantly go forth from the abominable Vanity, for the Fire thereof burneth.

THE THIRD CHAPTER.

Of the lamentable Fall of Man, and of the Means of his Deliverance.

NOW when Adam and Eve fell into this Vanity, then the Wrath of Nature awoke in each Property, and in or through the Desire impressed the Vanity of the Earthliness and Wrath of God into itself.

68. And then the Flesh became gross and rough, as the Flesh of a Beast, and the Soul was captivated in that Essence therewith, and saw that its Body was become a Beast, and had gotten the Bestial Members for Multiplication, and the filthy Carcase into which the Desire would stuff the Loathsomeness which it was ashamed of in the Presence of God; and therefore Adam and Eve hid themselves under the Trees of the Garden of Eden. Heat and Cold also seized on them.

69. And here the Heaven in Man trembled for Horror; as the Earth quaked in Wrath, when this Anger was destroyed on the Cross by the sweet Love of God; there the Anger trembled before the sweet Love of God.

70. And for this Vanity's Sake which was thus awakened in Man, God cursed the Earth; lest the holy Element should spring or shine forth any more through the outward Fruit, and bring forth Paradisaical Fruit. For there was then no Creature that could have enjoyed it; neither was the earthly Man worthy of it any more.

71. God would not cast the precious Pearls before Beasts; an ungodly Man in his Body being but a mere gross beastial Creature; and though it be of a noble Essence, yet it is wholly poisoned and loathsome in the Sight of God.

72. Now when God saw that his fair Image was spoiled, he manifested himself to fallen Adam and Eve, and had Pity on them, and promised himself to them for an everlasting Possession, and that with his great Love in the received Humanity he would destroy the Power of the Serpentine Property, viz., of the Vanity

in the Wrath of God awakened in them. And this was the breaking of the Head of the Serpent, which he would perform, viz., he would destroy the dark Death, and subdue the Anger with his great Love.

73. And this Covenant of his Incarnation which was to come, he put into the Light of Life; to which Covenant the Jewish Sacrifices pointed as to a Mark or Limit, to which God had promised himself with his Love; for the Faith of the Jews entered into the Sacrifices and Offerings, and God s Imagination entered into the Covenant.

74. And the Offering was a Figure of the Restitution of that which Adam hath lost, and so God did expiate his Anger in the human Property, through the offering in the Limit of the Covenant.

75. In which Covenant the most holy sweet Name JESUS, proceeding out of the holy Name and great Power of JEHOVAH, had incorporated itself; so that he would again move and manifest himself in the Substance of the Heavenly World which disappeared in Adam, and kindle the holy divine Life therein again.

76. This Mark or Limit of the Covenant was propagated from Adam and his Children, from Man to Man, and did go through from one upon all, as Sin also and the awakened Vanity did go through from one upon all.

77. And it stood in the Promise of the Covenant at the End, in the Root of David in the Virgin Mary, who was, in the inward Kingdom of the hidden Humanity, (viz., of the Essentiality that disappeared as to the Kingdom of God) the Daughter of God s Covenant, but in the outward according to the natural Humanity, she was begotten by her true bodily Father Joachim and her true Mother Anna, out of the Essences and Substance of their Souls and Bodies, like all other Children of Adam; a true Daughter of Eve.

78. In this Mary from the Virgin (viz., the Wisdom of God) in the promised Limit of the Covenant, of which all the Prophets have prophesied. - the eternal Speaking Word, which created all

Things, did in the Fullness of Time move itself in the Name JESUS, according to its highest and deepest Love and Humility, and bring again living, divine, and heavenly Substantiality into the Humanity of the heavenly Part, which disappeared in Adam, and from which he died in Paradise, into the Seed of Mary, into the Tincture of Love, into that Property wherein Adam should have propagated himself in a magical and heavenly Manner, into the true Seed of the Woman, of heavenly Substantiality, which disappeared in Paradise.

79. And when the Divine Light in the Heavenly Essence was extinguished, the Word of God, viz., the Divine Power of the Understanding, did bring in Heavenly and living Substantiality, and awakened the disappeared Substantiality in the Seed of Mary, and brought it to Life.

80. And so now God's Substance, wherein He dwelleth and worketh, and the disappeared Substance of Man, are become one Person; for the Holy Divine Substantiality did anoint the disappeared; therefore that Person is called CHRISTUS, the Anointed of God.

81. And this is the dry Rod of Aaron, which blossomed and bare Almonds, and the true High Priest; and it is that Humanity of which Christ spake, saying, that He was come from Heaven and was in Heaven; and that no Man could ascend into Heaven but the Son of Man which is come from Heaven, and is in Heaven.

82. Now when he saith, He is come from Heaven, it is meant of the Heavenly Substance, the Heavenly Corporeality; for the Power and Virtue of God needeth no coming any whither, for it is every where altogether immeasurable and undivided. But Substance needeth coming; the Power or Virtue needeth to move itself, and manifest itself in Substance.

83. And that Substance entered into the human Substance, and received it; not that Part only of Heavenly Substantiality, which disappeared in Adam, but the whole human Essence in Soul and Flesh, according to all the three Worlds.

84. But he hath not received, or taken upon himself, the awakened or impressed Vanity, which the Devil, by his Imagination, brought into the Flesh, by which the Flesh did commit Sin; though he hath indeed taken upon him the awakened Forms of Life, as they were gone forth from their equal Agreement, each of them into its own Desire.

85. For therein lay our Infirmity, and the Death, which He was to drown with his Heavenly holy Blood. Herein he took upon himself all our Sins and Infirmities, also Death and Hell in the Wrath of God, and destroyed their Power in the human Properties.

86. The Wrath of God was the Hell into which the Spirit of Christ went, when He had shed that heavenly Blood into our outward human Blood, and tinctured it with the Love; thereby changing that Hell of the human Property into Heaven, and reducing the human Properties into equal Agreement, into the Heavenly Harmony.

THE FOURTH CHAPTER.

How we are born a-new; and how we may fall into God's Anger again.

NOW here we may rightly understand what our New-Birth, or Regeneration, is; and how we may become, and continue to be, the Temple of God; though in this Life's Time, according to the outward Humanity, we are sinful mortal Men.

88. Christ in the human Essence hath broken up and opened the Gates of our inward Heavenly Humanity, which was shut up in Adam; so that nothing is now wanting, but that the Soul draw its Will out of the Vanity of the corrupted Flesh, and bring it into this open Gate in the Spirit of Christ.

89. Great and strong Earnestness is required here; and not only a learning and knowing, but a real Hunger and Thirst after the Spirit of Christ. For to know only, is not Faith; but an Hunger and Thirst after that which I want, so that I draw it in thereby to myself, and lay hold on it with the Desire and Imagination, and, make it my own; this is the Truth and Essence of a Christian's Faith.

90. The Will must go forth from the Vanity of the Flesh, and willingly yield itself up to the Suffering and Death of Christ, and to all the Reproach of Vanity, which derideth it, because it goeth forth from its own House wherein it was born, and regardeth Vanity no more, but merely desireth the Love of God in Christ Jesus.

91. In such a Hunger and Desire the Will receiveth and impresseth into itself the Spirit of Christ with his Heavenly Corporality; that is, the Soul in its great Hunger and Desire taketh hold of, and draweth the Body of Christ, viz., the Heavenly Substantiality, into its disappeared Image, within which the Word of the Power of God is the Working.

92. The Hunger of the Soul bringeth its Desire quite through the bruised Property of its Humanity in the Heavenly Part, which disappeared in Adam; which Humanity, the sweet Fire of Love in the Death of Christ did bruise, when the Death of that Heavenly Humanity was destroyed.

93. And so the Hunger of the Soul received into it, into its disappeared Corporality, through the Desire, the holy Heavenly Substance, viz., Christ s Heavenly Corporality, which filleth the Father all over, and is nigh unto all, and through all Things; and through that the disappeared Heavenly Body riseth in the Power of God, in the sweet Name JESU..

94. And this raised Heavenly Spiritual Body is the Member of Christ, and the Temple of the Holy Ghost, a true Mansion of the Holy Trinity, according to Christ s Promise, saying, We will come to you, and make our Abode in you.

95. The Essence of that Life eateth the Flesh of Christ, and drinketh his Blood. For the Spirit of Christ, viz., the Word, which made itself visible with the Humanity of Christ out of, and in our disappeared Humanity, through the outward Man of the Substance of this World, swalloweth its holy Substance into its fiery; for every Spirit eateth of its own Body.

96. Now if the Soul eat of this sweet, holy, and Heavenly Food, then it kindleth itself with the great Love in the Name and Power of JESUS; whence its Fire of Anguish becometh a great Triumph of Joy and Glory, and the true Sun ariseth to it, wherein it is born to another Will.

97. And here cometh to pass the Wedding of the Lamb, which we heartily wish that the titular and Lip-Christians might once find by Experience in themselves, and so pass from the History into the Substance.

98. But the Soul obtaineth not this Pearl of the Divine Wisdom and Virtue for its own Property during the Time of this Life; because it hath the outward Bestial Flesh sticking to its outward Man.

99. The Power of which Pearl of Divine Wisdom espouseth itself in this Wedding of the Lamb, and sinketh itself down into

the Heavenly Image, viz., into the Substance of the Heavenly Man, who is the Temple of Christ; and not into the Fire-Breath of the Soul, which is yet, during this whole Life's Time, fast bound to the outward Kingdom, to the Bond of Vanity, with the Breath of the Air, and is in great Danger.

100. It darteth its Beams of Love indeed very often into the Soul, whereby the Soul receiveth Light; but the Spirit of Christ yieldeth not itself up to the Fire-Breath in this Life's Time, but to the Breath of Light only which was extinguished in Adam, in which the Temple of Christ is, for that is the true and holy Heaven.

101. Understand aright now, what the New-Birth or Regeneration is, and how it cometh to pass, as followeth. The outward earthly mortal Man is not born anew in this Life's Time; that is, neither the outward Flesh, nor the outward Part of the Soul. They continue both of them in the Vanity of their Wills which awoke in Adam. They love their Mother, in whose Body they live, viz., the Dominion of this outward World; and therein the Birth of Sin is manifest.

102. The outward Man in Soul and Flesh, (we mean the outward part of the Soul) hath no Divine Will, neither doth he understand any Thing of God, as the Scripture saith, The natural Man perceiveth not the Things of the Spirit of God. &c.

103. But the Fire-Breath of the inward World, if it be once enlightened, understandeth it; it hath a great Longing, Sighing, Hunger, and Thirst after the sweet Fountain of Christ; it refresheth itself by hungering and desiring, (which is the true Faith in) the sweet Fountain of Christ from his new Body, from the Heavenly Substantiality, as a hungry Branch in the Vine Christ.

104. And the Reason why the fiery Soul cannot attain to Perfection during this Life's Time, is because it is fast bound with the outward Bond of Vanity, through which the Devil continually casteth his venomous Rays of Influence upon it, and so sifteth it, that it often biteth at his Bait, and poisoneth itself. From whence Misery and Anguish arise, so that the Noble Sophia hideth herself

in the Fountain of Christ, in the Heavenly Humanity; for she cannot draw near to Vanity.

105. For she knew how it went with her in Adam, when she lost her Pearl, which is of Grace freely bestowed again upon the inward Humanity; therefore she is called Sophia, viz., the Bride of Christ.

106. Here she faithfully calleth to her Bridegroom the fiery Soul, and exhorteth him to Repentance, and to the unburthening of himself, or going forth from the Abomination of Vanity.

107. And now War assaulteth the whole Man. The outward fleshly Man fighteth against the inward spiritual Man, and the spiritual against the fleshly; and so Man is in continual Warfare and Strife, full of Trouble, Misery, Anguish, and Care.

108. The inward Spirit saith to the fiery Soul: O my Soul! O my love! Turn I beseech thee and go forth from Vanity, or else thou loseth my Love and the noble Pearl.

109. Then saith the outward Reason, viz., the Beastial Soul; Thou art foolish; wilt thou be a Laughing-stock, and the Scorn of the World? Thou needest the outward World to maintain this Life. Beauty, Power, and Glory are thy proper Happiness; wherein only thou canst rejoice and take Delight. Why wilt thou cast thyself into Anguish, Misery, and Reproach? Take thy Pleasure, which will do both thy Flesh and thy Mind good.

110. With such Filth the true Man is often defiled; that is, the outward Man defileth himself, as a Sow in the Mire, and obscureth his noble Pearl. For the more vain the outward Man groweth, the more dark the inward Man cometh to be, until at length it disappeareth altogether.

111. And then the fair Paradisaical Tree is gone, and it will be very hard to recover it again. For when the outward Light, viz., the outward Soul is once enlightened, so that the outward Light of Reason is kindled by the inward Light; then the outward Soul commonly useth to turn Hypocrite, and esteem itself Divine, even though the Pearl be gone; which lamentable Error sticketh hard to many a Man.

112. And thus it comes to pass that the Tree of Pearl in the Garden of Christ is often spoiled; concerning which the Scripture maketh a hard Knot or Conclusion, viz., That those who have once tasted the Sweetness of the World to come, and fall away from it again, shall hardly see the Kingdom of God.

113. And though it cannot be denied, but that the Gates of Grace still stand open, yet the false and dazzling Light of the outward Reason of the Soul so deceiveth and hindereth such Men, that they suppose they have the Pearl, while they yet live to the Vanity of this World, and dance with the Devil after his Pipe.

THE FIFTH CHAPTER.

How a Man may call himself a Christian, and how not.

HERE therefore a Christian should consider why he calleth himself a Christian, and examine truly whether he be one or not. For surely my learning to know and confess that I am a Sinner, and that Christ hath destroyed my Sins on the Cross, and shed His Blood for me, doth not make me a Christian.

115. The Inheritance belongeth only to the Children. A Maid-Servant in a House knoweth well enough what the Mistress would have to be done, and yet that maketh her not the Heiress of her Mistress's Goods. The very Devils know that there is a God, yet that doth not change them into Angels again. But if the Maid-Servant in the House shall be married to the Son of her Mistress, then she may come to inherit her Mistress's Goods. And so it is to be understood also in the Matter of being a Christian.

116. The Children of the History are not the Heirs of the Goods of Christ, but the legitimate Children regenerated by the Spirit of Christ are the only true Heirs. For God said to Abraham, Cast out the Son of the Bondwoman, he shall not inherit with the Son of the Free. For he was a Scorner, and but an Historical Son of the Faith and Spirit of Abraham; and so long as he continued such a one, he was not a true Inheritor of the Faith of Abraham, and therefore God commanded he should be cast out from inheriting his Goods.

117. This was a Type of the future Christendom. For the Promise of Christendom was made to Abraham: Therefore the Type was then also set forth by two Brethren, Isaac and Ishmael; foreshewing by them the diverse State and Manners of Christendom; how that two sorts of Men would be in it, viz., True Christians and Lip-Christians. Which latter, under the Title or outward Profession of Christianity, would be but mockers, as Ishmael was and Esau, who also was a Type of the outward Adam, as Jacob was a Type of Christ, and His true Christendom.

118. Thus every one who will call himself a Christian, must cast out from himself the Son of the Bond-Woman, that is, the earthly Will, and be evermore killing and destroying it, and not settle it in the Inheritance.

119. Nor give the Pearl to the Beastial Man, for him to please and amuse himself with in the outward Light, in the Lust of the Flesh. But we must, with our Father Abraham bring the Son of the right Will to Mount Moriah, and be ready in Obedience to God to offer it up, ever in Will dying from Sin in the Death of Christ, giving no place to the Beast of Vanity in the Kingdom of Christ, nor letting it grow wanton, proud, covetous, envious, and malicious. For all these are the Properties of Ishmael the Son of the Bond-Woman whom Adam begat in his Vanity on the wanton Whore the false Bond-Woman, by the Devil s Imagination, out of the earthly Property in Flesh and Blood.

120. This Mocker and titular Christian is the Son of the false Bond-Woman, and must be cast out; for he shall not possess the Inheritance of Christ in the Kingdom of God. He is not fit, he is but Babel, a Confusion of that one Language into many. He is but a Talker and a Wrangler about the Inheritance; he means to get it to himself by Talking and Wrangling, by the Hypocrisy of his Lips and seeming Holiness, although in his Heart he is no better than a blood-thirsty Murderer of his brother Abel, who is the right Heir.

121. Therefore we say what we know, that he that will call himself a true Christian must try himself, and find what Kind of Properties drive and rule him, whether the Spirit of Christ moveth him to Truth and Righteousness, and to the Love of his Neighbour, so that he would willingly do what is right if he knew but how.

122. Now if he find that he hath a real Hunger after such Virtue, then he may justly think that he is drawn. And then he must begin to practise accordingly, and not be content with a Will only, without Doing. The drawing of the Father to Christ consisteth in the Will, but the true Life consisteth in the Doing; for the right Spirit doeth that which is right.

123. But if there be the Will to do, and yet the Doing followeth not, then the true Man is still shut up in vain Lust, which suppresseth the Doing. And therefore such a one is but an Hypocrite and an Ishmaelite; he speaketh one Thing and doth another, and witnesseth thereby that his Mouth is a Lyar; for he himself doth not that which he teacheth, and consequently only serveth the Beastial Man in Vanity.

124. For he that will say, I have a Will, and would willingly do Good, but the earthly Flesh which I carry about me, keepeth me back, so that I cannot; yet I shall be saved by Grace, for the Merits of Christ. I comfort myself with His Merit and Sufferings; who will receive me of mere Grace, without any Merits of my own, and forgive me my Sins. Such a one, I say, is like a Man that knoweth what Food is good for his Health, yet will not eat of it, but eateth Poison instead thereof, from whence Sickness and Death, will certainly follow.

125. For what good doth it to the Soul to know the Way to God, if it will not walk therein, but go on in a contrary Path? What good will it do the Soul to comfort itself with the Filiation of Christ, with His Passion and Death, and so flatter itself with the Hopes of getting the Patrimony thereby, if it will not enter into the Filial Birth, that it may be a true Child, born out of the Spirit of Christ, out of His Suffering, Death and Resurrection? Surely, the tickling and flattering itself with Christ's Merits, without the true innate Childship, is Falsehood and a Lie, whosoever he be that teacheth it.

126. This Comfort belongeth only to the penitent Sinner, who striveth against Sin and the Anger of God. When Temptations come, and the Devil assaulteth such a poor repentant Soul, then it must wholly wrap itself up in the Merits and Death of Christ, as its sole Armour of Defence.

127. Christ alone indeed hath merited Redemption for us; but not in such a Way as that for His own proper Merit s Sake, he will freely grant us his Childship by an outward Adoption only, and so receive us for Children, when we are none. No,. he himself is the Merit; he is the open Gate that leadeth through Death; and

through that Gate we must enter. He receiveth no Beast into his Merit, but those only that turn, and become as Children. Those Children that thus come to him are his Reward, which he hath merited.

128. For thus he said, Father, the Men were thine and thou hast given them to me (as my Reward) and I will give them eternal Life. But the Life of Christ will be given to none, unless they come to him in his Spirit, into his Humanity, Sufferings, and Merit, and therein be born true Children of the Merit.

129. We must be born of his Merit, and put on the Merit of Christ in his Passion and Death; not outwardly with verbal Flattery only, and bare comforting of ourselves therewith, while we still remain Aliens and strange Children, of a strange Essence or Nature. No; the strange Essence inheriteth not the Childship, but the innate Essence inheriteth it.

130. This innate Essence is not of this World, but in Heaven, of which St Paul speaketh saying, Our Conversation is in Heaven. The filial Essence walketh in Heaven, and Heaven is in Man.

131. But if Heaven in Man be not open, and the Man stand without Heaven flattering himself, and say, I am still without, but Christ will take me in through his Grace; is not his Merit mine? Such a one is in Vanity and Sin with the outward Man, and with the Soul in Hell, viz., in the Anger of God.

132. Therefore learn to understand rightly what Christ hath taught us, and done for us. He is our Heaven; he must get a Form in us, or else we shall not be in Heaven. Thus then the Soul's inward Man, with the holy Body of Christ, viz., in the New Birth, is in Heaven, and the outward mortal Man is in the World, of which Christ spake saying, My Sheep are in my Hand, and none shall pluck them away; the Father which gave them to me is greater than all.

THE SIXTH CHAPTER.

Of the right and of the wrong going to Church, receiving the Sacraments, and Absolution.

BELOVED Brethren, we will teach you faithfully, not with flattering Lips to please the Antichrist, but from our Pearl, the Virtue, Power, and Spirit of Christ in us, from a Christian Essence and Knowledge; not from the Husk and History, but from a New-born Spirit, from Christ's Knowledge, as a Branch growing on the Vine Christ; from the Measure of that Knowledge which is opened in us, according to the Will and Counsel of God.

134. Men tie us in these Days to the History, and to the material Churches of Stone; which Churches are indeed good in their Kind, if Men did also bring the Temple of Christ into them. They teach moreover, that their Absolution is a Forgiving of Sins, and that the Supper of the Lord taketh away Sin: Also that the Spirit of God cometh into Men through their Ministry. All which hath a proper Meaning, if it was rightly understood; and if Men did not cleave merely to the Husk.

135. Many a Man goeth to Church twenty or thirty Years, heareth Sermons, receiveth the Sacraments, and heareth Absolution read or declared, and yet is as much a Beast of the Devil and Vanity at the last as at the first. A Beast goeth into the Church, and to the Supper, and a Beast cometh out from thence again.

136. How will he eat that hath no Mouth? Can any Man eat that Food which is so shut up that he cannot get it? How will he drink that can come at no Water? Or how will he hear that hath no Hearing?

137. What good End doth it answer, for me to go to the material Churches of Stone, and there fill my Ears with empty Breath? or to go to the Supper, and feed nothing but the earthly Mouth, which is mortal and corruptible? Cannot I feed and satisfy that with a Piece of Bread at Home? What good doth it to the Soul, which is an immortal Life, to have the Beastial Man

observe the Form, and venerate the Shell of Christ s Institution, if it cannot obtain the Kernel thereof? For St Paul saith of the Supper, - You receive it to Condemnation, because ye discern not the Lord's Body.

138. The Covenant stands firm, and is stirred in the Use of the Institution. Christ proffereth his Spirit to us in His Word (viz., in his preached Word) and His Body and Blood in the Sacrament, and His Absolution in a brotherly Reconciliation one to another.

139. But what good doth it in a Beast to stand and listen, who hath no Hearing to receive the inward living Word, nor any Ground wherein to lay the Word, that it may bring forth Fruit? Of such Christ saith, The Devil plucketh the Word out of their Hearts, lest they should believe and be saved. But how can he do so? Because the Word findeth no Place in the hearing Mind to take Root in.

140. And thus it is with Absolution also: What Benefit is it to me for one to say, I pronounce or declare to thee the Forgiveness of thy Sins, when my Soul is wholly shut up in Sin? Whosoever saith thus to a Sinner so shut up, erreth; and he that receiveth it without the Voice of God within himself confirming the same, deceiveth himself. None can forgive Sins but God only.

141. The Preacher hath not Forgiveness of Sins in his own Power; but it is the Spirit of Christ in the Voice of the Priest that hath the Power, provided the Priest himself is a Christian.

142. What good did it to those that heard Christ himself teaching on Earth, when he said, Come unto me all ye that are weary and heavy laden, and I will give you Rest ? What good did this blessed Promise to those that heard it, if they laboured not, nor were heavy laden? What became of the Refreshment or Rest then? Seeing they had dead Ears, and heard only the outward Christ, and not the Word of the Divine Power; certainly they were not refreshed. Just so much good the Beastial Man hath of his Absolution and Sacraments.

143. The Covenant is open in the Sacraments; and in the Office or Ministry of teaching also the Covenant is stirred; the

Soul doth receive it, but in that Property only of which the Mouth of the Soul is.

144. That is, the outward Beast receiveth Bread and Wine, which it may have as well at Home. And the fiery Soul receiveth the Testament according to its Property, viz., in the Anger of God it receiveth the Substance of the eternal World, but according to the Property of the dark World; it receiveth therefore, as the Scripture saith, to its own Judgement or Condemnation. For as the Mouth is, so is the Food which is taken in by the Mouth. And after this Manner also it is that the Wicked shall behold Christ at the last Judgement as a severe Judge; but the Saints shall behold him as a loving Immanuel.

145. God s Anger standeth open in his Testaments towards the Wicked; but towards the Saints the heavenly loving Kindness, and in it the Power of Christ in the holy Name JESUS, standeth open. What good then doth the holy Thing do to the Wicked, who cannot enjoy it? Or what is there, that can take away his Sins, when his Sin is only stirred and made manifest thereby?

146. The Sacraments do not take away Sin; neither are Sins forgiven thereby. But it is thus: When Christ ariseth, then Adam dyeth in the Essence of the Serpent; as when the Sun riseth, the Night is swallowed up in the Day, and the Night is no more: Just so are Sins forgiven.

147. The Spirit of Christ eateth of his Holy Substance, the inward Man is the Receiver of the Holy Substance; he receiveth what the Spirit of Christ bringeth into him viz., the Temple of God, Christ s Flesh and Blood. But what doth this concern a Beast? Or what doth it concern the Devils? Or the Soul that is in the Anger of God? These eat of the Heavenly Blood, that is in the Heaven wherein they dwell, which is the Abyss, or bottomless Pit.

148. And thus it is also in the Office or Ministry of Preaching: The ungodly Man heareth what the outward Soul of the outward World preacheth; that he receiveth, viz., the History; and if there be Straw or Stubble in that which is taught, he sucketh the Vanity out of that. Yea, if the Preaching be mere Calumny, Railing, and uncharitable Abuse, as is sometimes the

Case, then his Soul sucketh the venomous Poison, and the murdering Cruelty of the Devil from it, wherewith it tickleth itself, and is pleased with learning how to judge and condemn others.

149. Thus if the Preacher be one that is dead, and hath no true Life in him, but soweth only Venom and Reproach proceeding out of his evil Affections, then it is the Devil that teacheth, and the Devil that heareth. Such teaching is received into a wicked heart, and bringeth forth wicked Fruits. By which Means the World is become a mere Den of murdering Devils. So that if you look among the Herd of such Teachers and Hearers, there is little to be found but Revilings, Slanderings, and Reproachings; together with Contention about Words, and Wrangling about the Husk.

150. But the Holy Ghost teacheth in the holy Teachers, and the Spirit of Christ heareth through the Soul, which is the Divine House of the Divine Sound or Voice in the holy Hearer.

151. The holy Man hath his Church in himself, wherein he heareth and teacheth. But Babel hath a Heap of Stones, into which she goeth with her seeming Holiness and real Hypocrisy. There she loved to be seen in fine Clothes, and maketh a very devout and godly Shew; the Church of Stone is her God, in which she putteth her Confidence.

152. But the holy Man hath his Church about him every where, even in himself; for he always standeth and walketh, sitteth and lyeth down in his Church. He liveth in the true Christian Church; yea, in the Temple of Christ. The Holy Ghost preacheth to him out of every Creature. Whatsoever he looketh upon, he seeth a Preacher of God therein.

153. Here now the Scoffer will say that I despise the Church Of Stone, where the Congregation meeteth; but I say that I do not. For I do but discover the hypocritical Whore of Babylon, which committeth Whoredom with the Church of Stone, and termeth herself a Christian, but is indeed a Strumpet.

154. A true Christian brings his holy Church with him into the Congregation. For the Heart is the true Church, where a Man

must practise the Service of God. If I should go a thousand Times to Church, and to the Sacrament every Week, and hear Absolution declared to me every Day, and have not Christ in me, all would be false, an unprofitable Fiction and graven Image in Babel, and no forgiving of Sins.

155. A holy Man doth holy Works from the holy Strength of his Mind. The Work is not the Atonement of Reconciliation, but it is the Building which the true Spirit buildeth in his Substance; it is his Habitation. But the Fiction and Fancy is the Habitation of the false Christian, into which his Soul entereth with Dissimulation. The outward Hearing reacheth but to the outward, and worketh in the outward only; but the inward Hearing goeth into the inward, and worketh in the inward.

156. Dissemble, roar, cry, sing, preach, and teach as much as thou wilt; yet if thine inward Teacher and Hearer be not open, all is nothing but a Babel a Fiction, and a graven Image, whereby the Spirit of the outward World doth model and make to itself a graven Image in Resemblance of the inward; and maketh a Holy Shew therewith, as if he performed some divine or holy Service to God; whereas many Times in such Service and Worship, the Devil worketh mightily in the Imagination, and very much tickleth the Heart with those Things wherein the Flesh delighteth. Which indeed not seldom happeneth to the Children of God, as to their outward Man, if they do not take great Heed to themselves; so busily doth the Devil beset and sift them.

THE SEVENTH CHAPTER.

Of unfprofitable Opinions, and Strife about the Letter.

A true Christian, who is born a-new of the Spirit of Christ, is in the Simplicity of Christ, and hath no Strife or Contention with any Man about Religion. He hath Strife enough in himself, with his own Beastial evil Flesh and Blood. He continually thinketh himself a great Sinner, and is afraid of God: But the Love of Christ by degrees pierceth through, and expelleth that Fear, as the Day swalloweth up the Night.

159. But the Sins of the impenitent Man rest in the Sleep of Death, bud forth in the Pit, and produce their Fruit in Hell.

160. The Christiandom that is in Babel, striving about the Manner how Men ought to serve God, and glorify him; also how they are to know him, and what he is in his Essence and Will. And they preach positively, that whosoever is not one and the same with them in every Particular of Knowledge and Opinion, is no Christian, but a Heretick.

161. Now I would fain see how all their Sects can be brought to agree in that one which might be called a true Christian Church; when all of them are Scorners, every Party of them reviling the rest, and proclaiming them to be false.

162. But a Christian is of no Sect: He can dwell in the midst of Sects, and appear in their Services, without being attached or bound to any. He hath but one Knowledge, and that is, Christ in him. He seeketh but one Way, which is the Desire always to do and teach that which is right; and he putteth all his knowing and willing into the Life of Christ.

163. He sigheth and wisheth continually that the Will of God might be done in him, and that his Kingdom might be manifested in him. He daily and hourly killeth Sin in the Flesh; for the Seed of the Woman, viz., the inward Man in Christ, continually breaketh the Head of the Serpent, that is, the Power of the Devil, which is in Vanity.

164. His Faith is a Desire after God and Goodness; which he wrappeth up in a sure Hope, trusting to the Words of the Promise, and liveth and dieth therein; though as to the true Man, he never dieth.

165. For Christ saith, Whosoever believeth in me, shall never die, but hath pierced through from Death to Life; and Rivers of living Water shall flow from him, viz., good Doctrine and Works.

166. Therefore I say, that whatsoever fighteth and contendeth about the Letter, is all Babel. The Letters of the Word proceed from, and stand all in, one Root, which is the Spirit of God; as the various Flowers stand all in the Earth and grow about one another. They fight not with each other about their Difference of Colour, Smell, and Taste, but suffer the Earth, the Sun, the Rain, the Wind, the Heat and Cold, to do with them as they please; and yet every one of them groweth in its own peculiar Essence and Property.

167. Even so it is with the Children of God; they have various Gifts and Degrees of Knowledge, yet all from one Spirit. They all rejoice at the great Wonders of God, and give Thanks to the most High in His Wisdom. Why then should they contend about him in whom they live and have their Being, and of whose Substance they themselves are?

168. It is the greatest Folly that is in Babel for People to strive about Religion, as the Devil hath made the World to do; so that they contend vehemently about Opinions of their own forging, viz., about the Letter; when the Kingdom of God consisteth in no Opinion, but in Power and Love.

169. As Christ said to his Disciples, and left it with them at the last, saying, Love one another, as I have loved you; for thereby Men shall know, that ye are my Disciples. If Men would as fervently seek after Love and Righteousness as they do after Opinions, there would be no Strife on Earth, and we should be as Children of One Father, and should need no Law, or Ordinance.

170. For God is not served by any Law, but only by Obedience. Laws are for the Wicked, who will not embrace Love

and Righteousness; they are, and must be, compelled and forced by Laws.

171. We all have but one only Order, Law, or Ordinance, which is to stand still to the Lord of all Beings, and resign our Wills up to him, and suffer His Spirit to play what Musick he will. And thus we give to him again as His own Fruits, that which he worketh and manifesteth in us.

172. Now if we did not contend about our different Fruits, Gifts, Kinds and Degrees of Knowledge, but did acknowledge them in one another, like Children of the Spirit of God, what could condemn us? For the Kingdom of God consisteth, not in our knowing and supposing, but in Power.

173. If we did not know half so much, and were more like Children, and had but a brotherly Mind and good Will, towards one another, and lived like Children of one Mother, and as Branches of one Tree, taking our Sap all from one Root, we should be far more holy than we are.

174. Knowledge serves only to this End, viz., to know that we have lost the Divine Power, in Adam, and are become now inclined to Sin; that we have evil Properties in us, and that doing Evil pleaseth not God; so that with our knowledge we might learn to do right. Now if we have the Power of God in us, and desire with all our Hearts to act and to live aright, then our Knowledge is but our Sport, or Matter of Pleasure, wherein we rejoice.

175. For true Knowledge is the Manifestation of the Spirit of God through the Eternal Wisdom. He knoweth what He will in His Children; He showeth his Wisdom and Wonders by his Children, as the Earth putteth forth its various Flowers.

176. Now if we dwell one with another, like humble Children, in the Spirit of Christ, one rejoicing at the Gift and Knowledge of another, who would judge or condemn us? Who judgeth or condemneth the Birds in the Woods, that praise the Lord of all Beings with various Voices, every one in its own Essence? Doth the Spirit of God reprove them for not bringing their Voices into one Harmony? Doth not the Melody of them all proceed from His power, and do they not sport before Him.

177. Those Men therefore that strive and wrangle about the Knowledge and Will of God, and despise one another on that Account, are more foolish than the Birds in the Woods, and the wild Beasts that have no true Understanding. They are more unprofitable in the Sight of the holy God than the Flowers of the Field, which stand still in quiet Submission to the Spirit of God, and suffer him to manifest the Divine Wisdom and Power through them. Yea, such Men are worse than Thistles and Thorns that grow among fair Flowers, for they at least stand still and are quiet, whereas those Wranglers are like the ravenous Beasts and Birds of Prey, which fright the other Birds from singing and praising God.

178. In short; they are the Issue, Branches or Sprouts of the Devil in the Anger of God, who, notwithstanding must by their very tormenting be made to serve the Lord; for by their plaguing and persecuting, they press out the Sap through the Essence in the Children of God, so that they move and stir themselves in the Spirit of God, with praying and continual sighing, in which Exercise of their Powers the Spirit of God moveth himself in them.

179. For thereby the Desire is exerted, and so the Children of God grow green, flourish, and bring forth Fruit; for the Children of God are manifested in Tribulation; as the Scripture saith, When thou chastiseth them, they cry fervently to thee.

THE EIGHTH CHAPTER.

Wherein Christian Religion consisteth; and how Men should serve God and their Brethren.

ALL Christian Religion wholly consisteth in this, to learn to know ourselves; whence we are come, and what we are; how we are gone forth from the Unity into Dissension, Wickedness, and Unrighteousness; how we have awakened and stirred up these Evils in us; and how we may be delivered from them again, and recover our original Blessedness.

181. First, how we were in the Unity, when we were the Children of God in Adam before he fell. Secondly, how we are now in Dissension and Disunion, in Strife and Contrariety. Thirdly, Whither we go when we pass out of this corruptible Condition; whither with the immortal, and whither with the mortal Part.

182. And Lastly, how we may come forth from Dis-union and Vanity, and enter again into that one Tree, Christ in us, out of which we all sprung in Adam. In these four Points all the necessary Knowledge of a Christian consisteth.

183. So that we need not strive about any Thing; we have no Cause of Contention with each other. Let every one only exercise himself in learning ahow he may enter again into the Love of God and his Brother.

184. The Testaments of Christ are nothing else but a loving Bond or brotherly Covenant, wherewith God in Christ bindeth himself to us and us to him. All teaching, willing, living, and doing, must imply, aim at, and refer to that. All teaching and doing otherwise, whatsoever it be, is Babel and a Fiction; a mere graven Image of Pride in unprofitable Judgings, a disturbing of the World, and an Hypocrisy of the Devil, wherewith he blindeth Simplicity.

185. Every Preacher void of the Spirit of God, who without Divine Knowledge, setteth himself up for a Teacher of Divine Things, pretending to serve God thereby, is false, and doth but

serve the Belly, his Idol, and his own proud insolent Mind, in desiring to be honoured on that Account, and esteemed Holy, or a Divine in Holy Orders. He beareth an Office, to which he is set apart and chosen by the Children of Men, who do but flatter him, and for Favour have ordained him thereunto.

186. Christ said, Whosoever entereth not by the Door, that is, through his Spirit, into the Sheepfold, but climbeth up some other Way, the same is a Thief and a Murderer, and the Sheep follow him not, for they know not his Voice.

187. He hath not the Voice of the Spirit of God, but the Voice of his own Art and Learning only; the Man teacheth, and not the Spirit of God. But Christ saith, Every Plant which my Heavenly Father hath not planted, shall be plucked up by the Roots.

188. How then will he that is ungodly plant Heavenly Plants, when he hath no Seed alive in its Power in himself? Christ saith expressly, The Sheep hear not his Voice, they follow him not.

189. The written Word is but an Instrument whereby the Spirit leadeth us to itself within us. That Word which will teach, must be living in the literal Word. The Spirit of God must be in the literal Sound, or else none is a Teacher of God, but a mere Teacher of the Letter, a Knower of the History, and not of the Spirit of God in Christ.

190. All that Men will serve God with, must be done in Faith, viz., in the Spirit. It is the Spirit that maketh the Work perfect, and acceptable in the Sight of God. All that a Man undertaketh and doeth in Faith, he doth in the Spirit of God, which Spirit of God doth cooperate in the Work, and then it is acceptable to God. For he hath done it himself, and his Power and Virtue is in it: It is holy.

191. But whatsoever is done in Self, without Faith, is but a Figure and Shell, or Husk of a true Christian Work.

192. If thou servest thy brother, and doest it but in Hypocrisy, and givest him unwillingly, then thou servest not God. For thy Faith proceedeth not from Love, nor entereth into Hope, in thy Gift. Indeed thou servest thy Brother, and he for his Part

thanketh God and blesseth thee, but thou blessest not him. For thou givest him thy Gift with a grudging Spirit, which entereth not into the Spirit of God, into the Hope of Faith; therefore thy Gift is but half given, and thou hast but half thy Reward for it.

193. The same is true of receiving a Gift. If any giveth in Faith, in Divine Hope, he blesseth his Gift by his Faith: But whoso receiveth it unthankfully, and murmureth in his Spirit, he curseth it in the Use or Enjoyment of it. Thus it is, that every one shall have his own; Whatsoever he soweth, that shall he also reap.

194. So likewise it is in the Office of teaching; whatsoever a Man soweth, that also he reapeth. For if any Man sow good Seed from the Spirit of Christ, it sticketh in the good Heart, and bringeth forth good Fruit; but in the Wicked, who are not capable of receiving the good Seed, the Anger of God is stirred.

195. If any sow Contentions, Reproaches, and Misconstructions, all ungodly People receive that unto them; which sticketh in them also, and bringeth forth Fruit accordingly. So that they learn thereby to despise, revile, slander, and misrepresent one another. Out of which Root the great Babel is sprung and grown; wherein Men, from mere Pride and Strife, contend about the History, and the Justification of a poor Sinner in the Sight of God; thereby causing the simple to err and blaspheme, insomuch that one Brother revileth and curseth the other, and excommunicateth, or casteth him to the Devil, for the Sake of the History and Letter.

196. Such Railers and Revilers fear not God, but raise the great Building of Dissension. And seeing corrupt Lust lieth in all Men, in the earthly Flesh still, therefore they raise and awaken Abominations even in the simple Children of God, and make the People of God, as well as the Children of Iniquity, to blaspheme. And thus they become Master-Builders of the great Babel of the World, and are as useful in the Church, as a fifth Wheel in a Waggon; yea, what is worse than that, they erect the hellish Building too.

197. Therefore it is highly necessary for the Children of God to pray earnestly, that they may learn to know this false

Building, and go forth from it with their Minds, and not help to build it up, and persecute their Fellow-Children of God. For by that Means they keep themselves back from the Heavenly Kingdom, and turn aside from the right Way.

198. According to the saying of Christ to the Pharisees, Woe unto you Pharisees; for you compass Sea and Land to make one Proselyte, and when he is one, you make him two-fold more the Child of Hell than yourselves. Which is truly too much the Case with the modern Factions and Sects among these Cryers and Teachers of Strife.

199. I desire therefore, out of my Gifts, which are revealed to me from God, that all the Children of God, who desire to be the true Members of Christ, be faithfully warned to depart from such abominable Contentions and bloody Firebrands, and to go forth from all Strife with their Brethren, and strive only after Love and Righteousness towards all Men.

200. For he that is a good Tree must bring forth good Fruits, and must sometimes suffer Swine to devour his Fruits, and yet must continue a good Tree still, and be always willing to work with God, and not suffer any Evil to overcome him. And then he standeth and groweth in the Field of God, and bringeth forth Fruit to be set upon God s Table, which he shall enjoy forever. Amen, All that hath Breath, praise the Name of the Lord. Hallelujah.

THE SUPER SENSUAL LIFE

by
Jacob Boehm 1575-1624,
The Teutonic Theosopher

TWO
DIALOGUES
BETWEEN
A DISCIPLE AND HIS MASTER,
CONCERNING
THE LIFE WHICH IS ABOVE SENSE.
SHOWING

How the Soul may attain to Divine HEARING and VISION - to a life above sense; and What its Childship in the Natural and Supernatural Life is; and How it passeth out of Nature into God, and out of God into Nature and Self again; also What its Salvation and Perdition are and What is the Partition Wall that separates the Soul from God and How the Breaking down of this Partition is effected; of the two Wills and two Eyes within the Fallen Soul; and What is the shortest WAY to the attainment of the Internal Kingdom of God and Why so few Souls do find It.

Composed by a Soul that loveth all
who are Children of JESUS CHRIST, under the Cross.

Brought forth in the 1600's by a humble shoemaker; translated into English over 100 years later; suppressed and hidden away until recently in theological archives around the world... a worthy personal study not just for academics but for all those who are spiritually grounded in the WORD, who are learning to hear the Lord, and who hunger for more.

Dear Reader

I Corinthians 2, 7-15: We speak the hidden mystical Wisdom of God, which God ordained before the World unto our Glory; Which none of the Princes of this World knew; For had they known it, they would not have crucified the Lord of Glory. But, as it is written, Eye hath not seen, nor Ear heard, neither hath it entered into the Heart of man to conceive the Things which God hath prepared for them that Love him. But God hath revealed them unto us by His Spirit: For the Spirit searcheth all Things, yea, the deep Things of God. For what Man knoweth the Things of a Man, save the Spirit of a Man which is in him? Even so the Things of God knoweth no Man, but the Spirit of God. Now we have received, not the Spirit of this World, but the Spirit which is of God; that we might know the Things that are freely given us of God. Which Things also we speak, not in the Words which Man's Wisdom teacheth, but which the Holy Ghost teacheth; comparing Spiritual Things with Spiritual. But the natural Man receiveth not the Things of the Spirit of God: For they are Foolishness unto him; neither can he know them, because they are Spiritually discerned. But he that is Spiritual judgeth, or discerneth all Things.

OF
THE SUPERSENSUAL LIFE
OR
THE LIFE WHICH IS ABOVE SENSE
IN
Two DIALOGUES between a disciple and his Master

THE FIRST DIALOGUE

The Disciple said to his Master: Sir, How may I come to the Place that I may SEE with God, and may HEAR God speak - to a Life that is above my Senses and Feelings - to the Supersensual Life?

The Master answered and said: Son, when thou canst throw thyself into THAT, where no Creature dwelleth, though it be but for a Moment, then thou HEAREST what God speaketh.

Disciple:
Is that Place where no Creature dwelleth near at Hand; or is it afar off?

Master:
It is IN THEE. And if thou canst, my Son, for a while but cease from all thy OWN Thinking and Willing, then thou shalt hear the unspeakable Words of God.

Disciple:
How is it that I can hear Him speak, when I stand still from Thinking and Willing?

Master:
When thou standest still from the Thinking of SELF, and the Willing of SELF; when both thy Intellect and Will are quiet and passive to the Impressions of the Eternal Word and Spirit; when thy Soul is winged up, and above that which is temporal with the outward Senses and the Imagination being locked up by Holy Abstraction; then the Eternal Hearing, Seeing, and Speaking

will be revealed IN THEE; and so God heareth and seeth through thee, being now the Organ of His Spirit; and so God speaketh in thee, and whispereth to thy Spirit, and thy Spirit heareth his Voice. Blessed art thou therefore if that thou canst stand still from SELF-Thinking and SELF-Willing, and canst stop the Wheel of thy Imagination and Senses; for it is hereby that thou mayest arrive at Length to see the great Salvation of God, being made capable of all Manner of Divine Sensations and Heavenly Communications. Since it is nought indeed but thine OWN Hearing and Willing that do hinder thee, so that thou dost not see and hear God.

Disciple:

But wherewith shall I hear and see God, for as much as He is above Nature and Creature?

Master:

Son, when thou art quiet and silent, then art thou as God was before Nature and Creature; thou art that which God then was; thou art that whereof He made thy Nature and Creature: Then thou hearest and seest even with that wherewith God Himself saw and heard in thee, before ever thine OWN Willing or thine OWN Seeing began.

Disciple:

What now hinders or keeps me back, so that I cannot come to that, wherewith God is to be seen and heard?

Master:

Nothing truly but thine OWN Willing, Hearing, and Seeing do keep thee back from it, and do hinder thee from coming to this Supersensual State or the Life which is above Sense. And it is because thou strivest so against that, out of which thou thyself art descended and derived, that thou thus breakest thyself off, with thine OWN Willing, from God's Willing, and with thine OWN Seeing from God's Seeing. In as much as in thine OWN Seeing thou dost see in thine OWN Willing only, and with thine OWN Understanding thou dost understand but in and according to this thine OWN Willing, as the same stands divided from the Divine Will. This thy Willing moreover stops thy Hearing, and maketh thee deaf towards God, through thy OWN Thinking upon terrestrial Things, and thy Attending to that which is without thee; and so it brings thee into a Ground, where thou art laid hold on and captivated in Nature. And having brought thee hither, it overshadows thee with that which thou willest; it binds thee with thine own Chains, and it keeps thee in thine own dark Prison which thou makest for thyself; so that thou canst not go out thence, or come to that State which is above Nature and above Sense.

Disciple:

But being I am in Nature, and thus bound, as with my own Chains, and by my own natural Will; pray be so kind, Sir, as to tell me, how I may come through Nature into the Supersensual and Supernatural Ground, without the destroying of Nature?

Master:

Three Things are requisite in order to do this. The First is, Thou must resign up thy Will to God; and must sink thy SELF down to the Dust in His Mercy. The Second is, Thou must hate thy OWN Will, and forbear from doing that to which thy own Will doth drive thee. The Third is, Thou must bow thy Soul under the Cross, heartily submitting thySELF to It, that thou mayest be able to bear the Temptations of Nature and Creature. And if thou doest thus, know that God will speak into thee, and will bring thy resigned Will in to Himself, in the supernatural Ground; and then thou shalt hear, my Son, what the Lord speaketh in thee.

Disciple:

This is a hard Saying, Master; for I must forsake the World, and my Life too, if I should do thus.

Master:

Be not discouraged hereat. If thou forsakest the World, then thou comest into that out of which the World is made; and if thou losest thy Life, then thy Life is in that, for whose Sake thou forsakest it. Thy Life is in God, from whence it came into the Body; and as thou comest to have thine OWN Power faint and weak and dying, the Power of God will then work in thee and through thee.

Disciple:

Nevertheless as God hath created Man in and for the natural Life, to rule over all Creatures on Earth, and to be a Lord over all Things in this World, it seems not to be at all unreasonable, that Man should therefore possess this World, and the Things therein for his own.

Master:

If thou rulest over all Creatures but outwardly, there cannot be much in that. But if thou hast a Mind to possess all Things, and to be a Lord indeed over all Things in this World, there is quite another Method to be taken by thee.

Disciple:

Pray, how is that? And what Method must I take, whereby to arrive at this Sovereignty?

Master:

Thou must learn to distinguish well betwixt the Thing, and that which only is an Image thereof; betwixt that Sovereignty which is substantial, and in the inward Ground or Nature, and that which is imaginary, and in an outward Form, or Semblance; betwixt that which is properly Angelical, and that which is no more than bestial. If thou rulest now over the Creatures externally only, and not from the right internal Ground of thy renewed Nature; then thy Will and Ruling is verily in a bestial Kind or Manner, and thine at best is but a Sort of imaginary and transitory Government, being void of that which is substantial and permanent, the which only thou art to desire and press after. Thus by thy outwardly Lording it over the Creatures, it is most easy for thee to lose the Substance and the Reality, while thou hast nought remaining but the Image or Shadow only of thy first and original Lordship; wherein thou art made capable to be again invested, if thou wouldest be but wise, and takest thy Investiture from the Supreme Lord in the right Course and Manner.

Whereas by thy willing and ruling thus after a bestial Manner, thou bringest also thy Desire into a bestial Essence, by which Means thou becomest infected and captivated therein, and gettest therewith a bestial Nature and Condition of Life. But if thou shalt have put off the bestial and ferine Nature, and if thou hast left the imaginary Life, and quitted the low imaged Condition of it; then art thou come into the Super-Imaginariness, and into the intellectual Life, which is a State of living above Images, Figures and Shadows. And so thou rulest over all Creatures, being reunited with thine Original, in that very Ground or Source, out of which they were and are created; and henceforth Nothing on Earth can hurt thee. For thou art like all Things and Nothing is unlike thee.

Disciple:

O loving Master, pray teach me how I may come the shortest Way to be like unto All Things.

Master:

With all my Heart. Do but think on the Words of our Lord Jesus Christ, when He said, "Except ye be converted, and become as little Children, ye shall not enter into the Kingdom of Heaven." There is no shorter Way than this; neither can there be a better Way found. Verily, Jesus saith unto thee, Unless thou turn and become as a Child, hanging upon Him for All Things, thou shalt not see the Kingdom of God. This do, and Nothing shall hurt thee; for thou shalt be at Friendship with all the Things that are, as thou dependest on the Author and Fountain of them, and becomest like Him, by such Dependence, and by the Union of thy Will with His Will. But mark what I have further to say; and be not thou startled at it, though it may seem hard for thee at first to conceive. If thou wilt be like All Things, thou must forsake All Things; thou must turn thy Desire away from them All, and not desire or hanker after any of them; thou must not extend thy Will to possess that for thy own, or as thine own, which is Something, whatsoever that Something be.

For as soon as ever thou takest Something into thy Desire, and receivest it into thee for thine OWN, or in Propriety, then this very Something (of what Nature soever it is) is the same with thyself; and this worketh with thee in thy Will, and thou art thence bound to protect it, and to take Care of it even as of thy own Being. But if thou dost receive no Thing into thy Desire, then thou art free from All Things, and rulest over all Things at once, as a Prince of God. For thou hast received Nothing for thine own, and art Nothing to all Things; and all Things are as Nothing to thee. Thou art as a Child, which understands not what a Thing is, and though thou dost perhaps understand it, yet thou understandest it without mixing with it, and without its sensibly affecting or touching thy Perception, even in that Manner wherein God doth rule and see all Things; He comprehending All, and yet Nothing comprehending Him.

Disciple:

Ah! How shall I arrive at this Heavenly Understanding, at this Sight of All Things in God, at this pure and naked Knowledge which is abstracted from the Senses; at this Light above Nature and Creature; and at this Participation of the Divine Wisdom which oversees all Things, and governs through all intellectual Beings? For, alas, I am touched every Moment by the Things which are about me; and overshadowed by the Clouds and Fumes which rise up out of the Earth. I desire therefore to be taught, if possible, how I may attain such a State and Conditions as no Creature may be able to touch me to hurt me; and how my Mind, being purged from sensible Objects and Things, may be prepared for the Entrance and Habitation of the Divine Wisdom in me?

Master:

Thou desirest that I would teach thee how thou art to attain it; and I will direct thee to our Master, from Whom I have been taught it, that thou mayest learn it thyself from Him, Who alone teacheth the Heart. Hear thou Him. Wouldest thou arrive at this; wouldest thou remain untouched by Sensibles; wouldest thou behold Light in the very Light of God, and see all Things thereby; then consider the Words of Christ, Who is that Light; and Who is the Truth. O consider now His Words, Who said, "Without

Me ye can do nothing" and defer not to apply thyself unto Him, Who is the Strength of thy Salvation, and the Power of thy Life; and with Whom thou canst do all Things, by the Faith which He worketh in thee. But unless thou wholly givest thySELF up to the Life of our Lord Jesus Christ, and resignest thy Will wholly to Him, and desirest Nothing and willest Nothing without Him, thou shalt never come to such a Rest as no Creature can disturb. Think what thou pleasest, and be never so much delighted in the Activity of thine OWN Reason, thou shalt find that in thine OWN Power, and without such a total Surrender to God, and to the Life of God, thou canst never arrive at such a Rest as this, or the true Quiet of the Soul, wherein no Creature can molest thee, or so much as touch thee. Which when thou shalt, by Grace, have attained to, then with thy Body thou art in the World, as in the Properties of outward Nature; and with thy Reason, under the Cross of our Lord Jesus Christ; but with thy Will thou walkest in Heaven, and art at the End from whence all Creatures are proceeded forth, and to which they return again. And then thou canst in this END, which is the same with the BEGINNING, behold all Things outwardly with Reason, and inwardly with the Mind; and so mayest thou rule in all Things and over all Things, with Christ; unto Whom all Power is given both in Heaven and on Earth.

Disciple:
O Master, the Creatures which live in me do withhold me, that I cannot so wholly yield and give up mySELF as I willingly would. What am I to do in this Case?

Master:
Let not this trouble thee. Doth thy Will go forth from the Creatures? Then the Creatures are forsaken in thee. They are in the World, and thy Body, which is in the World, is with the Creatures. But spiritually thou walkest with God, and conversest in Heaven, being in thy Mind redeemed from Earth, and separated from Creatures, to live the Life of God. And if thy Will thus leaveth the Creatures, and goeth forth from them, even as the Spirit goeth forth from the Body at Death; then are the Creatures

dead in it, and do live only in the Body in the World. Since if thy Will doth not bring itself into them, they cannot bring themselves into it, neither can they by any Means touch the Soul. And hence St. Paul saith,"Our Conversation is in Heaven"; and also, "Ye are the Temple of God, and the Spirit of God dwelleth in you." So then True Christians are the very Temples of the Holy Ghost, Who dwelleth in them; that is, the Holy Ghost dwelleth in the Will, and the Creatures dwelleth in the Body.

Disciple:

If now the Holy Spirit doth dwell in the Will of the Mind, how ought I to keep myself so that He depart not from me again?

Master:

Mark, my Son, the Words of our Lord Jesus Christ; "If ye abide in My Words, then My Words abide in you." If thou abideth with thy Will, in the Words of Christ; then His Word and Spirit abideth in thee, and all shall be done for thee that thou canst ask of Him. But if thy Will goeth into the Creature, then thou hast broken off thereby thyself from Him. And then thou canst not any otherwise keep thyself but by abiding continually in the most resigned Humility, and by entering into a constant Course of Penitence, wherein thou wilt be always grieved at thine own Creatureliness and that Creatures do still live in thee, that is, in thy bodily Appetites. If thou doest thus, thou standest in a daily dying from the Creatures, and in a daily ascending into Heaven in thy Will; which Will is also the Will of thy Heavenly Father.

Disciple:

O my loving Master, pray teach me how I may come to such a constant Course of holy Penitence, and to such a daily Dying from all creaturely Objects; for how can I abide continually in Repentance?

Master:

When thou leavest that which loveth thee, and lovest that which hateth thee; then thou mayest abide continually in Repentance.

Disciple:

What is it that I must thus leave?

Master:

All Things that love and entertain thee, because thy Will loves and entertains them; all Things that please and feed thee, because thy Will feeds and cherishes them; all Creatures in Flesh and Blood; in a Word, all Visibles and Sensibles, by which either the Imagination or sensitive Appetite in Men are delighted and refreshed. These the Will of thy Mind, or thy supreme Part must leave and forsake; and must even account them all its Enemies. This is the Leaving of what loves thee. And the Loving of what hates thee, is the Embracing of the Reproach of the World. Thou must learn then to love the Cross of the Lord Jesus Christ, and for His Sake to be pleased with the Reproach of the World which hates and derides thee; and let this be thy daily Exercise of Penitence - to be crucified to the World, and the World to thee. And so thou shalt have continual Cause to hate thySELF in the Creature, and to seek the Eternal Rest which is in Christ. To which Rest thou having thus attained, thy Will may therein safely rest and repose itself, according as thy Lord Christ hath said: "In Me ye may have Rest, but in the World ye shall have Anxiety; In Me ye may have Peace, but in the World ye shall have Tribulation."

Disciple:

How shall I now be able to subsist in this Anxiety and Tribulation arising from the World, so as not to lose the Eternal Peace, or not enter into this Rest? And how may I recover myself in such a Temptation as this is, by not sinking under the World, but rising above it by a Life that is truly Heavenly or Supersensual?

Master:

If thou dost once every Hour throw thyself by Faith beyond all Creatures, beyond and above all sensual Perception and Apprehension, yea, above Discourse and Reasoning into the abyssal Mercy of God, into the Sufferings of our Lord, and into the Fellowship of His Interceding, and yieldeth thySELF fully and absolutely thereinto; then thou shalt receive Power from above to rule over Death and the Devil, and so subdue Hell and the World under thee: And then thou mayest subsist in all Temptations, and be the brighter for them.

Disciple:

Blessed is the Man that arriveth to such a State as this. But alas! Poor Man that I am, how is this possible as to me? And what, O my Master, would become of me, if I should ever attain with my Mind to that, where no Creature is? Must I not cry out, I am undone!

Master:

Son why art thou so dispirited? Be of good Heart still; for thou mayest certainly yet attain to it. Do but believe, and all Things are made possible to thee. If it were that thy Will, O thou of little Courage, could break off itself for one Hour, or even but for one half Hour, from all Creatures, and plunge itself into That where no Creature is, or can be; presently it would be penetrated and clothed upon with the supreme Splendor of the Divine Glory, would taste in itself the most sweet Love of Jesus, the Sweetness whereof no Tongue can express, and would find in itself the unspeakable Words of our Lord concerning His great Mercy. Thy Spirit would then feel in itself the Cross of our Lord Jesus Christ to be very pleasing to it; and would thereupon love the Cross more than the Honors and Goods of the World.

Disciple:

This for the Soul would be exceeding well indeed: But what would then become of the Body seeing that it must of Necessity live in the Creature?

Master:

The Body would by this Means be put into the Imitation of our Lord Christ, and of His Body: It would stand in the Communion of that most blessed Body, which was the true Temple of the Deity; and in the Participation of all its gracious Effects, Virtues and Influences. It would live in the Creature not of Choice, but only as it is made subject unto Vanity, and in the World, as it is placed therein by the Ordination of the Creator, for its Cultivation and the higher Advancement; and as groaning to be delivered out of it in God's Time and Manner, for its

Perfection and Resuscitation in Eternal Liberty and Glory, like unto the Glorified Body of our Lord and His risen Saints.

Disciple:

But the Body being in its present Constitution, so made subject to Vanity, and living in a vain Image and creaturely Shadow, according to the Life of the undergraduated Creatures or Brutes, whose Breath goeth downwards to the Earth; I am still very much afraid thereof, lest it should continue to depress the Mind which is lifted up to God, by hanging as dead Weight thereto; and go on to amuse and perplex the Same, as formerly, with Dreams and Trifles, by letting in the Objects from without, in order to draw me down into the World and the Hurry thereof; where I would fain maintain my Conversation in Heaven, even while I am living in the World. What therefore must I do with this Body, that I may be able to keep up so desirable a Conversation; and not to be under any Subjection to it any longer?

Master:

There is no other Way for thee that I know, but to present the Body whereof thou complainest (which is the Beast to be sacrificed) "a living Sacrifice, holy and acceptable unto God": And this shall be thy "rational Service", whereby this thy Body will be put, as thou desirest, into the Imitation of Jesus Christ, who said, His Kingdom was not of this World. Be not thou then "conformed to it, but be transformed by the Renewing of thy Mind"; which renewed Mind is to have Dominion over the Body, that so thou mayest prove, both in Body and Mind, what is the perfect Will of God, and accordingly perform the same with and by his Grace operating IN THEE. Whereupon the Body, or the Animal Life would, being thus offered up, begin to die, both from without and from within. From without, that is, from the Vanity and evil Customs and Fashions of the World. It would be an utter Enemy to all the Pomp thereof, and to all the Gaudery, Pageantry, Pride, Ambition, and Haughtiness therein. From within, it would die as to all the Lusts and Appetites of the Flesh, and would get a Mind and Will wholly new, for its Government and Management; being now made subject to the Spirit, which would continually be directed to God, as would all that is subject to thy Body. And thus thy very Body is become the Temple of God and of His Spirit, in Imitation of thy Lord's Body.

Disciple:

But the World would hate it, and despise it for so doing; seeing it must hereby contradict the World, and must live and act quite otherwise than the World doth. This is most certain. And how can this then be taken?

Master:

It would not take that as any Harm done to it, but would rather rejoice that it is become worthy to be like unto the Image of our Lord Jesus Christ, being transformed from that of the World: And it would be most willing to bear that Cross after our Lord; merely that our Lord might bestow upon it the Influence of His sweet and precious Love.

Disciple:

I do not doubt but in some this may be even so. Nevertheless for my own Part, I am in a Straight betwixt two, not feeling yet enough of that blessed Influence upon me. O how willingly should my Body bear that, could this be safely depended upon by me, according to what is urged! Wherefore pardon me, loving Sir, in this one Thing, if my Impatience doth still further demand what would become of it, if the Anger of God from within, and the wicked World also from without, should at once assault it, as the same really happened to our Lord Christ?

Master:

Be that unto it, even as unto our Lord Christ, when He was reproached, reviled and crucified by the World; and when the Anger of God so fiercely assaulted Him for our Sake. Now what did He do under this most terrible Assault both from without and from within? Why, He commended his Soul into the Hands of his Father, and so departed from the Anguish of this World into the Eternal Joy. Do thou likewise; and His Death shall become thy Life.

Disciple:

Be it unto me as unto the Lord Christ; and unto my Body as unto His; which into His Hands I have commended, and for the Sake of His Name do offer up, according to His revealed Will. Nevertheless I am desirous to know what would become of my Body in its pressing forth from the Anguish of this miserable World into the Power of the Heavenly Kingdom?

Master:

It would get forth from the Reproach and Contradiction of the World, by a Conformity to the Passion of Jesus Christ; and from the Sorrows and Pains in the Flesh, which are only the Effects of some sensible Impression of Things without, by a quiet Introversion of the Spirit, and secret Communion with the Deity manifesting Itself for that End. It would penetrate into itself; it would sink into the great Love of God; it would be sustained and refreshed by the most sweet name JESUS; and it would see and find within itself a new World springing forth as through the Anger of God, into the Love and Joy Eternal. And then should a Man wrap his Soul in this, even in the great Love of God, and clothe himself Therewith as with a Garment; and should account thence all Things alike; because in the Creature he finds NoThing that can give him, without God, the least Satisfaction; and because also Nothing of Harm can touch him more, while he remains in this Love, which indeed is stronger that all Things, and makes a Man hence invulnerable both from within and without, by taking out the Sting and Poison of the Creatures, and destroying the Power of Death. And whether the Body be in Hell or on Earth, all is alike to him; for whether it be there or here, his Mind is still in the greatest Love of God; which is no less than to say, that he is in Heaven.

Disciple:

But how would a Man's Body be maintained in the World; or how would he be able to maintain those that are his, if he should by such a Conversation incur the Displeasure of all the World?

Master:

Such a Man gets greater Favors than the World is able to bestow upon him. He hath God for his Friend; he hath all His Angels for his Friends: In all Dangers and Necessities these protect and relieve him; so that he need fear no Manner of Evil; no Creature can hurt him. God is his Helper; and that is sufficient. Also God is his Blessing in every Thing; and though sometimes it may seem as if God would not bless him, yet is this but for a Trial to him, and for the Attraction of the Divine Love; to the End he may more fervently pray to God, and commit all his Ways unto Him.

Disciple:

He loses however by this all his good Friends; and there will be none to help him in his Necessity.

Master:

Nay, but he gets the Hearts of all his true Friends into his Possession, and loses none but his Enemies, who before loved his Vanity and Wickedness.

Disciple:

How it is that he can get his true Friends into his Possession?

Master:

He gets the very Hearts and Souls of all those that belong to our Lord Jesus to be his Brethren, and the Members of his own very Life. For all the Children of God are but One in Christ, which One is Christ in All; and therefore he gets them all to be his Fellow Members in the Body of Christ, whence they have all the same Heavenly Goods in common; and all live in one and the same Love of God, as the Branches of a Tree in one and the same Root, and spring all from one and the same Source of Life in them. So that he can have no Want of spiritual Friends and Relations, who are all rooted with him together in the Love which is from above; who are all of the same Blood and Kindred in Christ Jesus; and who are all nourished by the same quickening Sap and Spirit diffusing Itself through them universally from the one True Vine, which is the Tree of Life and Love. These are Friends worth having; and though Here they may be unknown to him, will abide his Friends beyond Death, to all Eternity. But neither can he want even outward natural Friends, as our Lord Christ when on Earth did not want such also.

For though indeed the High-Priests and Potentates of the World could not have a Love for Him because they belonged not to Him, neither stood in any Kind of Relation to Him, since He was not of this World; yet those loved Him who were capable of His Love, and receptive of His Words. So in like Manner, those who love Truth and Righteousness will love that Man, and will associate themselves unto him, yea, though they may perhaps be outwardly at some Distance or seeming Disagreement, from the Situation of their worldly Affairs, or out of some certain Respects; yet in their Hearts they cannot but cleave to him. For though they be not yet actually incorporated into one Body with him, yet they cannot resist being of one Mind with him, and being united in Affection, for the great Regard they bear to the Truth, which shines forth in his Words and in his Life. By which they are made either his declared or his secret Friends; and he doth so get their Hearts, as they will be delighted above all Things in his Company, for the Sake thereof, and will court his Friendship, and will come unto him by Stealth, if openly they dare not, for the Benefit of his Conversation and Advice; even as Nicodemus did unto Christ, who came to Him by Night, and in his Heart loved Jesus for the Truth's Sake, though outwardly he feared the World. And thus thou shalt have many Friends that are not known to thee; and some known to thee, who may not appear so before the World.

Disciple:

Nevertheless it is very grievous to be generally despised of the World, and to be trampled upon by Men as the very Offscouring thereof.

Master:

That which now seems so hard and heavy to thee, thou wilt yet hereafter be most of all in Love with.

Disciple:

How can it be that I should ever love that which hates me?

Master:

Though thou lovest the earthly Wisdom now, yet when thou shalt be clothed upon with the Heavenly Wisdom, then thou wilt see that all the Wisdom of the World is Folly; and wilt see also that the World hates not so much thee, as it does thine Enemy, which is the Mortal Life. And when thou thyself shalt come to hate the Will thereof, by Means of a habitual Separation of thy Mind from the World, then thou also wilt begin to love that despising of the Mortal Life, and the Reproach of the World for Christ's Sake . And so shalt thou be able to stand under every Temptation, and to hold out to the End by the Means hereof in the Course of Life above the World, and above Sense. In this Course thou wilt hate thyself; and thou wilt also love thyself; I say love thyself, and that even more than ever thou didst yet.

Disciple:

But how can these two subsist together, that a Person should both love and hate himself?

Master:

In loving thyself, thou lovest not thySELF as thine OWN; but as given thee from the Love of God thou lovest the Divine Ground in thee; by which and in which thou lovest the Divine Wisdom, the Divine Goodness, the Divine Beauty; thou lovest also by it God's Works of Wonders; and in this Ground thou lovest likewise thy Brethren. But in hating thySELF, thou hatest only that which is thine OWN, and wherein the Evil sticks close to thee.

And this thou dost, that so thou mayest wholly destroy that which thou callest thine; as when thou sayest I or MYSELF do this, or do that. All which is wrong, and a downright Mistake in thee; for nothing canst thou properly call thine but the Evil SELF, neither canst thou do any Thing of thyself that is to be accounted of. This SELF therefore thou must labor wholly to destroy IN THEE, that so thou mayest become a Ground wholly Divine. There is, there can be no SELFishness in Love; they are opposite to each other. Love, that is, Divine Love (of which only we are now discoursing) hates all Egoity, hates all that which we call I, or IHOOD; hates all such Restrictions and Confinements, yea even all that springs from a contracted Spirit, or this evil SELF-hood, because it is a hateful and deadly Thing. And it is impossible that these two should stand together, or subsist in one Person; the one driving out the other by a Necessity of Nature. For Love possesses Heaven, and dwells in Itself, which is dwelling in Heaven; but that which is called I, this vile SELF-hood possesses the World and worldly Things; and dwells also in itself, which is dwelling in Hell, because this is the very Root of Hell itself. And therefore as Heaven rules above the World and as Eternity rules above Time, even so ought Love to rule above the natural temporal Life; for no other Method is there, neither can there be of attaining to that Life which is Supernatural and Eternal, and which thou so much desirest to be led into.

Disciple:

Loving Master, I am well content that this Love should rule in me over the natural Life, so that I may attain to that which is Supernatural and Supersensual; but pray tell me now, why must Love and Hatred, Friend and Foe thus be together? Would not Love alone be better? Wherefore, I say, are Love and Trouble thus joined?

Master:

If Love dwelt not in Trouble, It could have Nothing to love; but when Its Substance which It loves, namely, the poor Soul, is in Trouble and Pain, Love hath thence Cause to love this, Its own Substance, and to deliver it from its Pain; that so the Soul, itself, may by the indwelling Love be again Beloved. Neither could any one know what Love is, if there were no Hatred; or what Friendship is, if there were no Foe to contend with. Or in one Word, for Love to be known It must have Something which It might Love, and where Its Virtue and Power may be manifested, by working out Deliverance to the Beloved from all Pain and Trouble.

Disciple:

Pray what is the Virtue, Power, the Height and the Greatness of Love?

Master:

The Virtue of Love is NOTHING and ALL, or that Nothing visible out of which All Things proceed; Its Power is through All Things; Its Height is as high as God; Its Greatness is as great as God. Its Virtue is the Principle of all Principles; Its Power supports the Heavens and upholds the Earth; Its Height is higher than the highest Heavens; and Its Greatness is even greater than the very Manifestation of the Godhead in the glorious Light of the Divine Essence, as being infinitely capable of greater and greater Manifestations in all Eternity. What can I say more? Love is higher than the Highest. Love is greater than the Greatest. Yea, It is in a certain Sense greater than God; while yet in the highest Sense of all, God is Love, and Love is God. Love being the highest Principle, is the Virtue of all Virtues; from whence they all flow forth. Love being the greatest Majesty, is the Power of all Powers, from whence they severally operate; and It is the Holy Magical Root, or Ghostly Power from whence all the Wonders of God have been wrought by the Hands of his elect Servants, in all their Generations successively. Whosoever finds It, finds Nothing and All Things.

Disciple:

Dear Master, pray tell me how to understand this.

Master:

First then, in that I said, Its Virtue is Nothing, or that NOTHING which is the BEGINNING of All Things, thou must understand It thus; when thou art gone forth wholly from the Creature, and from that which is visible, and art become Nothing to all that is Nature and Creature, then thou art in that Eternal One, which is God Himself. And then thou shalt perceive and feel in thy Interior, the highest Virtue of Love. But in that I said, Its Power is through All Things, this is that which thou perceivest and findest in thy own Soul and Body experimentally, whenever this great Love is enkindled within thee; seeing that It will burn more than the Fire can do, as It did in the Prophets of old, and afterwards in the Apostles, when God conversed with them bodily, and when His Spirit descended upon them in the Oratory of Zion. Thou shalt then see also in all the Works of

God, how Love hath poured Itself into all Things, and penetrateth all Things, and is the most inward and most outward Ground in all Things - inwardly in the Virtue and Power of every Thing, and outwardly in the Figure and Form thereof.

And in that I said, Its Height is as high as God; thou mayest understand this in thyself; forasmuch as It brings thee to be as high as God Himself is, by being united to God - as may be seen by our beloved Lord Christ in our Humanity. Which Humanity Love hath brought up into the highest Throne, above all Angelical Principalities and Powers, into the very Power of the Deity itself.

But in that I also said, Its Greatness is as great as God, thou art hereby to understand, that there is a certain Greatness and Latitude of Heart in Love, which is inexpressible; for It enlarges the Soul as wide as the whole Creation of God. And this shall be truly experienced by thee, beyond all Words, when the Throne of Love shall be set up in thy Heart.

Moreover in that I said, Its Virtue is the Principle of all Principles, hereby it is given thee to understand, that Love is the principiating Cause of all created Beings, both spiritual and corporeal, by Virtue whereof the second Causes do move and act occasionally according to certain Eternal Laws from the Beginning implanted in the very Life and Energy of all the Principles of Nature, superior and inferior -It reaches to all Worlds, and to all Manner of Beings in them contained, they being the Workmanship of Divine Love; and It is the first Mover, and first Moveable both in Heaven above and in the Earth beneath, and in the Water under the Earth. And hence there is given to It the Name of Lucid Aleph, or Alpha; by which is expressed the Beginning of the Alphabet of Nature, and of the Book of Creation and Providence, or the Divine Archetypal Book, in which is the Light of Wisdom, and the Source of all Lights and Forms.

And in that I said, Its Power supports the Heavens; by this thou wilt come to understand, that as the Heavens, visible and invisible, are originated from this great Principle, so are they likewise necessarily sustained by It; and that therefore if This should be but never so little withdrawn, all the Lights, Glories, Beauties, and Forms of the heavenly Worlds, would presently sink into Darkness and Chaos.

And whereas I further said, that It upholds the Earth; this will appear to thee no less evident than the former, and thou shalt perceive It in thyself by daily and hourly Experience; forasmuch as the Earth without It, even thy own Earth also, (that is, thy Body) would certainly be without Form and Void. By the Power thereof the Earth hath been thus long upheld, notwithstanding a foreign usurped Power introduced by the Folly of Sin. And should this but once fail or recede, there could no longer be either Vegetation or Animation upon it; yea, the very Pillars of it would be quite overthrown, and the Band of Union, which is that of Attraction or Magnetism, called the Centripetal Power, being broken and dissolved, all must thence run into the utmost Disorder, and falling away as into Shivers, would be dispersed as loose Dust before the Wind.

But in that I said, Its Height is higher than the highest Heavens; this thou mayest also understand within thyself; so shouldest thou ascend in Spirit through all the Orders of Angels and heavenly Powers, yet the Power of Love still is undeniably superior to them all. And as the Throne of God, Who sits upon the Heaven of Heavens, is higher than the highest of them, even so must Love also be, which fills them all, and comprehends them all.

And whereas I said of the Greatness of Love, that It is greater than the very Manifestation of the Godhead in the Light of the Divine Essence; that is also true. For Love enters even into that where the Godhead is not manifested in this glorious Light, and where God may be said not to dwell. And entering thereinto, Love begins to manifest to the Soul the Light of the Godhead; and thus is the Darkness broken through, and the Wonders of the new Creation successively manifested.

Thus shalt thou be brought to understand really and fundamentally, what is the Virtue and Power of Love, and what the Height and Greatness thereof is; how that It is indeed the Virtue of all Virtues, though It be invisible, and as a Nothing in Appearance, inasmuch as It is the Worker of all Things, and a powerful vital Energy passing through all Virtues and Powers natural and supernatural; and the Power of all Powers, nothing being able to let or obstruct the Omnipotence of Love, or to resist Its invincible penetrating Might, which passes through the whole Creation of God, inspecting and governing all Things.

And in that I said, It is higher than the Highest, and greater than the Greatest; thou mayest hereby perceive as in a Glimpse, the supreme Height and Greatness of Omnipotent Love, which infinitely transcends all that human Sense and Reason can reach to. The highest Archangels and the greatest Powers of Heaven are, in Comparison of it, but as Dwarfs. Nothing can be conceived higher and greater in God Himself, by the very Highest and Greatest of His Creatures. There is such an Infinity in It, as comprehends and surpasses all the Divine Attributes.

But in that it was also said, Its Greatness is greater than God; that likewise is very true in the Sense wherein it was spoken; For Love, as I before observed, can there enter where God dwelleth not, since the most high God dwelleth not in Darkness, but in the Light - the hellish Darkness being put under His Feet. Thus for Instance, when our beloved Lord Christ was in Hell, Hell was not the Mansion of God or of Christ; Hell was not God, neither was it with God, nor could it be at all with Him; Hell stood in the Darkness and Anxiety of Nature, and no Light of the Divine Majesty did there enter. God was not there; for He is not in the Darkness or in the Anguish; but Love was there; and Love destroyed Death and conquered Hell. So also when thou art in Anguish or Trouble, which is Hell within, God is not the Anguish or Trouble; neither is He in the Anguish or Trouble; but His Love is there, and brings thee out of the Anguish and Trouble into God, leading thee into the Light and Joy of His Presence. When God hides Himself in thee, Love is still there, and makes Him manifest in thee. Such is the inconceivable Greatness and Largeness of Love; which will hence appear to thee as great as God above Nature, and greater than God in Nature, so as considered in his manifestative Glory.

Lastly, whereas I also said, Whosoever finds It, finds Nothing and All Things; that is also certain and true. But how finds he Nothing? Why, I will tell thee how. He that findeth it, findeth a Supernatural Supersensual Abyss, which hath no Ground or Byss to stand on, and where there is no Place to dwell in; and he findeth also Nothing is like unto It, and therefore It may fitly be compared to Nothing; for It is deeper than any Thing, and is as NoThing with respect to All Things, forasmuch as It is not comprehensible by any of them. And because It is NoThing respectively, It is therefore free from All Things; and is that only Good, which a Man cannot express or utter what It is; there being Nothing to which It may be compared, to express It by.

But in that I lastly said, Whosoever finds It, finds All Things; there is nothing can be more true than this Assertion. It hath been the BEGINNING of All Things; and It ruleth All Things. It is also the END of All Things; and will thence comprehend All Things within Its Circle. All Things are from It, and in It, and by It. If thou findest It, thou comest into that Ground from whence All Things are proceeded, and wherein they subsist; and thou art in It a KING over all the Works of God.

Here the Disciple was exceedingly ravished with what his Master had so wonderfully and surprisingly declared, and returned his most humble and hearty Thanks for that Light, which his Master had been an Instrument of conveying to him. But being desirous to hear further concerning these high Matters, and to know Somewhat more particularly, he requested him that he would give him Leave to wait on him the next Day again; and that he would then be pleased to show him how and where he might find this which was so much beyond all Price and Value, and whereabout the Seat and Abode of it might be in human Nature; with the entire Process of the Discovery and bringing it forth to Light.

The Master said to him: This then we will discourse about at our next Conference, as God shall reveal the same to us by his SPIRIT, which is the Searcher of All Things. And if thou dost remember well what I answered thee in the Beginning, thou shalt soon come thereby to understand that hidden mystical Wisdom of God, which none of the Wise Men of the World know; and where the MIND thereof is to be found in thee, shall be given thee from above to discern. Be silent therefore in thy Spirit, and watch unto Prayer; that when we meet again Tomorrow in the Love of Christ, thy Mind may be disposed for finding that noble PEARL, which to the World appears Nothing, but which to the Children of Wisdom is All Things.

THE SECOND DIALOGUE.

ARGUMENT

Herein is described and set forth the Manner of passing the Gulf which divides betwixt the two Principles or States of Heaven and Hell: And it is particularly shown how this Transaction is carried on in the Soul; what the Partition Wall therein is, which separates from God.

What the breaking down of this Partition Wall, and how effected; what the Center of Light is, and the pressing into that Center is; What the Light of God, and Light of Nature are; how they are operative in their several Spheres, and how to be kept from interfering with each other; with some Account of the two Wills and their Contraposition in the Fallen State; of the Magical Wheel of the Will, and how the Motion thereof may be regulated; of the Eye in the Midst thereof, what the Right Eye is to the Soul, and what the Left is, but especially what the Single Eye is, and in what Manner it is to be obtained; of the Purification from the Contagion of Matter; of the Destruction of Evil, and of the very Annihilation of it, by the Subsidence of the Will from its own Something into Nothing; of the Naked and Magical Faith, and the Attraction thereby of a certain Divine Substantiality and Vestment; how all consists in the Will, and proceeds but from one Point; where that Point is placed, and how it may be found out; and which is both the safest and nearest Way to attain to the high supersensual State, and the internal Kingdom of Christ, according to the true Heavenly Magia or Wisdom.

The Disciple being very earnest to be more fully instructed how he might arrive at the Supersensual Life; and how, having found All Things, he might come to be a King over all God's Works; came again to his Master the next Morning, having watched the Night in Prayer, that he might be disposed to receive and apprehend the Instructions that should be given him by a Divine Irradiation upon his Mind. And the Disciple after a little Space of Silence, bowed himself, and thus brake forth:

Disciple:

O my Master! my Master! I have now endeavoured to recollect my Soul in the Presence of God, and to cast myself into that Deep where no Creature doth nor can dwell; that I might hear the Voice of my Lord speaking in me; and be initiated into that high Life, whereof I heard Yesterday such great and amazing Things pronounced. But alas! I neither hear nor see as I should; there is still such a Partition Wall in me which beats back the Heavenly Sounds in their Passage, and obstructs the Entrance of that Light by which alone Divine Objects are discoverable, as till this be broken down, I can have but small Hopes, yea, even none at all, of arriving at those glorious Attainments which you pressed me to, or of entering into that where no Creature dwells, and which you call Nothing and All Things. Wherefore be so kind as to inform me what is required on my Part, that this Partition which hinders may be broken or removed.

Master:

This Partition is the Creaturely Will in thee; and this can be broken by nothing but by the Grace of SELF-DENIAL, which is the Entrance into the True Following of Christ, and totally removed by Nothing but a perfect Conformity with the Divine Will.

Disciple:

But how shall I be able to break this Creaturely Will which is at Enmity with the Divine Will? Or, what shall I do to follow Christ in so difficult a Path, and not to faint in a continual Course of SELF-DENIAL and RESIGNATION to the Will of God?

Master:

This is not to be done by thyself; but by the Light and Grace of God received into thy Soul, which will, if thou gainsay not, break the Darkness that is in thee, and melt down thine OWN Will, which worketh in the Darkness and Corruption of Nature, and bring it into the Obedience of Christ, whereby the Partition of the Creaturely SELF is removed from betwixt God and thee.

Disciple:

I know that I cannot do it of myself. But I would fain learn, how I must receive this Divine Light and Grace into me, Which is to do it for me, if I hinder It not my own SELF. What is then required of me in order to admit this Breaker of the Partition and to promote the Attainment of the Ends of such Admission?

Master:

There is Nothing more required of thee at first, than not to resist this Grace, Which is manifested in thee; and Nothing in the whole Process of thy Work, but to be obedient and passive to the Light of God shining through the Darkness of thy Creaturely Being, which reaching no higher than the Light of Nature, comprehendeth It not.

Disciple:

But is it not for me to attain, if I can, both the Light of God, and the Light of the outward Nature too; and to make use of them both for the ordering of my Life wisely and prudently?

Master:

It is right, I confess, so to do. And it is indeed a Treasure above all earthly Treasures, to be possessed of the Light of God and Nature, operating in their Spheres; and to have both the Eye of Time and Eternity at once open together, and yet not to interfere with each other.

Disciple:

This is a great Satisfaction to me to hear; having been very uneasy about it for some Time. But how this can be without interfering with each other, there is the Difficulty. Wherefore, fain would I know, if it were lawful, the Boundaries of the one and the other; and how both the Divine and the Natural Light may in their several Spheres respectively act and operate, for the Manifestation of the Mysteries of God and Nature, and for the Conduct of my outward and inward Life?

Master:

That each of these may be preserved distinct in their several Spheres, without confounding Things Heavenly and Things Earthly, or breaking the golden Chain of Wisdom, it will be necessary, my Child, in the first Place to wait for and attend the

Supernatural and Divine Light, as that superior Light appointed to govern the Day, rising in the true East, which is the Center of Paradise; and in great Might breaking forth as out of the Darkness within thee, through a Pillar of Fire and Thunder-Clouds, and thereby also reflecting upon the inferior Light of Nature a Sort of Image of Itself, whereby only it can be kept in its due Subordination; that which is below being made subservient to that which is above; and that which is without to that which is within. Thus there will be no Danger of interfering; but all will go right, and every Thing abide in its proper Sphere.

Disciple:

Therefore without Reason or the Light of Nature be sanctified in my Soul, and illuminated by this superior Light, as from the central East of the holy Light-World, by the Eternal and Intellectual Sun; I perceive there will always be some Confusion, and I shall never be able to manage aright either what concerneth Time or Eternity; but I must always be at a Loss, or break the Links of Wisdom's Chain.

Master:

It is even so as thou hast said. All is Confusion, if thou hast no more but the dim Light of Nature, or unsanctified and unregenerated Reason to guide thee by; and if only the Eye of Time be opened in thee, which cannot pierce beyond its own Limit. Wherefore seek the Fountain of Light, waiting in the deep Ground of thy Soul for the rising there of the Sun of Righteousness, whereby the Light of Nature in thee, with the Properties thereof, will be made to shine seven Times brighter than ordinary. For it shall receive the Stamp, Image, and Impression of the Supersensual and Supernatural; so that the sensual and rational Life will hence be brought into the most perfect Order and Harmony.

Disciple:

But how am I to wait for the Rising of this glorious Sun, and how am I to seek in the Center, this Fountain of Light, which may enlighten me throughout, and bring all my Properties into perfect Harmony? I am in Nature, as I said before; and which

Way shall I pass through Nature, and the Light thereof, so that I may come into that Supernatural and Supersensual Ground, from whence this true Light, which is the Light of Minds, doth arise; and this, without the Destruction of my Nature, or quenching the Light of it, which is my - Reason?

Master:

Cease but from thine own Activity, steadfastly fixing thine Eye upon one Point, and with a strong Purpose relying upon the promised Grace of God in Christ, to bring thee out of thy Darkness into His Marvelous Light. For this End gather in all thy Thoughts, and by Faith press into the Center, laying hold upon the Word of God, which is infallible, and which hath called thee. Be thou then obedient to this Call; and be silent before the Lord, sitting alone with Him in thy inmost and most hidden Cell, thy Mind being centrally united in itself, and attending His Will in the Patience of Hope. So shall thy Light break forth as the Morning; and after the Redness thereof is passed, the Son Himself, which thou waitest for, shall arise unto thee, and under His most healing Wings thou shalt greatly rejoice; ascending and descending in His bright and salutiferous Beams. Behold this is the true Supersensual Ground of Life.

Disciple:

I believe it indeed to be even so. But will not this destroy Nature? Will not the Light of Nature in me be extinguished by this greater Light? Or must not the outward Life hence perish, with the earthly Body which I carry?

Master:

By no Means at all. It is true, the evil Nature will be destroyed by It; but by the Destruction thereof you can be no Loser, but very much the Gainer. The Eternal Band of Nature is the same afterward as before; and the Properties are the same. So that Nature hereby is only advanced and meliorated; and the Light thereof, or human Reason, by being kept within its due Bounds, and regulated by a superior Light is only made useful.

Disciple:

Pray therefore let me know how this inferior Light ought to be used by me; how it is to be kept within its due Bounds; and after what Manner the superior Light doth regulate and ennoble it.

Master:

Know then, my beloved Son, that if thou wilt keep the Light of Nature within its own proper Bounds, and make use thereof in just Subordination to the Light of God; thou must consider that there are in thy Soul two Wills, an inferiour Will, which is for driving thee to Things without and below; and a superiour Will, which is for drawing to Things within and above. These two Wills are now set together, as it were, Back to Back, and in a direct Contrariety to each other; but in the Beginning, it was not so. For this Contraposition of the Soul in these two is no more than the Effect of the Fallen State; since before that they were placed one under the other, that is, the superiour Will Above, as the Lord, and the inferiour Below, as the Subject. And thus it ought to have continued.

Thou must also further consider, that answering to these two Wills there are likewise two Eyes in the Soul, whereby they are severally directed; forasmuch as these Eyes are not united in one single View, but look quite contrary Ways at once. They are in a like Manner set one against the other, without a common Medium to join them. And hence, so long as this Double-sightedness doth remain, it is impossible there should be any Agreement in the Determination of this or that Will. This is very plain; and it showeth the Necessity that this Malady, arising from the Dis-union of the Rays of Vision, be some Way remedied and redressed, in order to a true Discernment in the Mind. Both these Eyes therefore must be made to unite by a Concentration of Rays; there being nothing more dangerous than for the Mind to abide thus in the Duplicity, and not to seek to arrive at the Unity of Vision. Thou perceivest, I know, that thou hast two Wills in thee, one set against the other, the Superior and the Inferior; and that thou hast also two Eyes within, one against another; whereof the one Eye may be called the Right Eye, and the other the Left Eye.

Thou perceivest too, doubtless, that it is according to the Right Eye that the Wheel of the superiour Will is moved; and that it is according to the Left Eye, that the contrary Wheel in the lower is turned about.

Disciple:

I perceive this, Sir, to be very true; and this it is which causeth a continual Combat in me, and createth to me greater Anxiety than I am able to express. Nor am I unacquainted with the Disease of my own Soul, which you have so clearly declared. Alas! I feel such irregular and convulsive Motions drawing me on this Side and that Side. The Spirit seeth not as the Flesh seeth; neither doth, or can the Flesh seeth as the Spirit seeth. Hence the Spirit willeth against the Flesh; and the Flesh willeth against the Spirit in me. This hath been my hard Case. And how shall it be remedied? O how may I arrive at the Unity of Will, and how come into the Unity of Vision?

Master:

Mark now what I say: The Right Eye looketh forward in thee into Eternity. The Left Eye looketh backward in thee into Time. If now thou sufferest thyself to be always looking into Nature, and the Things of Time, and to be leading the Will, and to be seeking Somewhat for thyself in the Desire, it will be impossible for thee ever to arrive at the Unity, which thou wishest for. Remember this; and always be upon thy Watch. Give not thy Mind leave to enter into, nor to fill itself with, that which is without thee; neither look thou backward upon thySELF; but quit thySELF, and look forward upon Christ. Let not thy Left Eye deceive thee, by making continually one Representation after another, and stirring up thereby an earnest Longing in the SELF-Propriety; but let thy Right Eye command back this Left, and attract it to thee, so that it may not gad Abroad into the Wonders and Delights of Nature. Yea, it is better to pluck it quite out, and to cast it from thee, than to suffer it to proceed forth without Restraint into Nature, and to follow its own Lusts. However there is for this no Necessity, since both Eyes may become very useful, if ordered aright; and both the Divine and natural Light may in the Soul subsist together, and be of mutual Service to each other. But never shalt thou arrive at the Unity of Vision or Uniformity of Will, but by entering fully into the Will of our Saviour Christ, and therein bringing the Eye of Time into the Eye of Eternity; and then descending by Means of this united through the Light of God into the Light of Nature.

Disciple:

So then if I can but enter into the Will of my LORD, and abide therein, I am safe, and may both attain to the Light of God in the Spirit of my Soul, and see with the Eye of God, that is, the Eye of Eternity in the Eternal Ground of my Will; and may also at the same Time enjoy the Light of this World nevertheless; not degrading but adorning the Light of Nature; and beholding as with the Eye of Eternity Things Eternal, so with the Eye of Nature Things Natural, and both contemplating therein the Wonders of God, and sustaining also thereby the Life of my outward Vehicle or Body.

Master:

It is very right. Thou hast well understood; and thou desirest now to enter into the Will of God, and to abide therein as in the Supersensual Ground of Light and Life, where thou mayest in His Light behold both Time and Eternity, and bring all the Wonders created of God for the exterior into the interior Life, and so eternally rejoice in them to the Glory of Christ; the Partition of thy Creaturely Will being broken down, and the Eye of thy Spirit simplified in and through the Eye of God manifesting Itself in the Center of thy Life. Let this be so now, for it is God's Will.

Disciple:

But it is very hard to be always looking forwards into Eternity; and consequently to attain to this single Eye, and Simplicity of Divine Vision. The Entrance of a Soul naked into the Will of God, shutting out all Imaginations and Desires, and breaking down the strong Partition which you mention, is indeed somewhat very terrible and shocking to human Nature in its present State. O what shall I do, that I may reach this which I so much long for?

Master:

My Son, let not the Eye of Nature with the Will of the Wonders depart from that Eye which is introverted into the Divine Liberty, and into the Eternal Light of the holy Majesty; but let it draw to thee those Wonders by Union with that heavenly internal Eye, which are externally wrought out and manifested in visible Nature. For while thou art in the World, and hast an honest Employment, thou art certainly by the Order of Providence obliged to labor in it, and to finish the Work given thee, according to thy best Ability, without Repining or Complaining in the least and to seek out and manifest for God's Glory, the Wonders of Nature and Art. Since let the Nature be what it will, it is all the Work and Art of God; and let the Art also be what it will, it is still God's Work, and His Art, rather than any Art or Cunning of Man. And all both in Art and Nature serveth but abundantly to manifest the wonderful Works of God; that He for all, and in all may be glorified. Yea, all serveth but to recollect thee more inward if thou knowest rightly how to use them, and to draw thy Spirit into that majestic Light, wherein the original Patterns and Forms of Things visible are to be seen. Keep therefore in the Center, and stir not out from the Presence of God revealed within thy Soul; let the World and the Devil make never so great a Noise and Bustle to draw thee out, mind them not; they cannot hurt thee. It is permitted to the Eye of thy Reason to seek Food, and to thy Hands, by their Labor, to get Food for the terrestrial Body. But then this Eye ought not with its Desire to enter into the Food prepared, which would be Covetousness; but must in Resignation simply bring it before the Eye of God in thy Spirit, and then thou must seek to place it close to this very Eye, without letting it go. Mark this Lesson well.

Let the Hands or the Head be at Labor, thy Heart ought nevertheless to rest in God. God is a Spirit; dwell in the Spirit, work in the Spirit, pray in the Spirit, and do every Thing in the Spirit; for remember thou also art a Spirit, and thereby created in the Image of God. Therefore see that thy Desire attract not Matter unto thee, but as much as possible abstract thyself from all Matter whatever; and so, standing in the Center, present thyself as a vacant, naked Spirit before God, in Simplicity and Purity; and be sure thy Spirit draw in nothing but Spirit.

Thou wilt yet be greatly enticed to draw Matter, and to gather that which the World calls Substance, thereby to have somewhat visible to trust to. But by no Means consent to the Tempter, nor yield to the Lusting of thy Flesh against the Spirit. For in so doing thou wilt infallibly obscure the Divine Light in thee; thy Spirit will stick in the dark covetous Root, and from the fiery Source of thy Soul will it blaze out in Pride and Anger; thy Will shall be chained in Earthliness, and shall sink through the Anguish into Darkness and materiality; and never shalt thou be able to reach the still Liberty, or to stand before the Majesty of God. Since this is opening a Door for him who reigneth in the Corruption of Matter, possibly the Devil may roar at thee for this Refusal; because nothing can vex him worse than such a silent Abstraction of the Soul, and Controversion thereof to the Point of Rest from all that is worldly and circumferential. But regard him not; neither admit into thee the least Dust of Matter which he may pretend any Claim to. It will be all Darkness to thee, as much Matter as is drawn in by the Desire of thy Will. It will darken God's Majesty to thee; and will close the seeing Eye, by hiding from thee the Light of His beloved Countenance. This the Serpent longeth to do; but in vain, except thou permittest thy Imagination upon his Suggestion, to receive in the alluring Matter; else he can never get in. Behold then, if thou desirest to see God's Light in thy Soul, and be divinely illuminated and conducted, this is the short Way that thou art to take; not to let the Eye of thy Spirit enter into Matter, or fill itself with any Thing whatever, either in Heaven or Earth; but to let it enter by naked Faith into the Light of the Majesty; and so receive by pure Love the Light of God, and attract the Divine Power into itself, putting on the Divine Body, and growing up in it to the full Maturity of the Humanity of Christ.

Disciple:

As I said before, so I say again, this is very hard. I conceive indeed well enough that my Spirit ought to be free from the Contagion of Matter, and wholly empty, so that it may admit into it the Spirit of God. Also, that this Spirit will not enter, but where the Will entereth into Nothing, and resigneth itself up in the Nakedness of Faith, and in the Purity of Love, to Its Conduct; feeding magically upon the Word of God, and clothing itself thereby with a Divine Substantiality. But alas, how hard it is for the Will to sink into Nothing, to attract Nothing, to imagine Nothing!

Master:

Let it be granted that it is so. Is it not surely worth thy Time and Effort, and all that thou canst ever do?

Disciple:

It is so, I must needs confess.

Master:

But perhaps it may not be so hard as at first it appeareth to be; make but the Trial, and be in earnest. What is there required of thee, but to stand still, and see the Salvation of thy God? And couldst thou desire any Thing less? Where is the Hardship in this? Thou hast Nothing to care for, Nothing to desire in this Life, Nothing to imagine or attract. Thou needest only cast thy Care upon God, who careth for thee, and leave Him to dispose of thee according to His Good Will and Pleasure, even as if thou hadst no Will at all in thee. For He knoweth what is best; and if thou canst but trust Him, He will most certainly do better for thee, than if thou were left to thine own Choice.

Disciple:

This I most firmly believe.

Master:

If thou believest, then go and do accordingly. All is in the Will, as I have shown thee. When the Will imagineth after Somewhat, then entereth it into that Somewhat, then presently that same Somewhat taketh the Will into itself, and overcloudeth it, so that it can have no Light, but must dwell in Darkness, unless it return back out of that Somewhat into Nothing. For when the Will imagineth or lusteth after Nothing, then it entereth into Nothing, where it receiveth the Will of God into itself, and so dwelleth in Light, and worketh all its Works in that Light.

Disciple:

I am now satisfied that the Main Cause of any one's Spiritual Blindness is his letting his Will into Somewhat, or into that which he hath wrought, of what Nature soever it be, Good or Evil, and his setting his Heart and Affections upon the Work of his own Hands or Brain; and that when the earthly Body perisheth, then the Soul must be imprisoned in that very Thing which it shall have received and let in; and if the Light of God be not in it, being deprived of the Light of this World, it cannot but be found in a dark Prison.

Master:

This is a very precious Gate of Knowledge; I am glad thou takest it into such Consideration. The understanding of the whole Scripture is contained in it; and all that hath been written from the Beginning of the World to this Day, may be found herein, by him that having entered with his Will into Nothing, hath there found All Things by finding God; from Whom, and to Whom, and in Whom are All Things. By this Means thou shalt come to hear and see God; and after this earthly Life is ended, to see with the Eye of Eternity all the Wonders of God and of Nature, and more particularly those which shall have been wrought by thee in the Flesh, or all that the Spirit of God shall have given thee to labor out for thyself and thy Neighbor, or all that the Eye of Reason enlightened from above, may at any Time have manifested to thee. Delay not therefore to enter in by this Gate, which if thou seest in the Spirit, as some highly favored Souls have seen it, thou seest in the Supersensual Ground, all that God is, and can do; thou seest also therewith, as one hath said who was taken thereinto, through Heaven, Hell, and Earth, and through the Essence of all Essences. Whosoever findeth It, hath found All that he can possibly desire. Here is the Virtue and Power of the Love of God displayed. Here is the Height and Depth; here is the

Breadth and Length thereof manifested, as ever the Capacity of thy Soul can contain. By this thou shalt come into that Ground out of which all Things are originated, and in which they subsist; and in It thou shalt reign over all God's Works, as a Prince of God.

Disciple:
Pray tell me, dear Master, where dwelleth It in Man?
Master:
Where Man dwelleth not, there It hath Its Seat in Man.
Disciple:
Where is that in a Man, where Man dwelleth not in himself?
Master:
It is the resigned Ground of a Soul, to which NoThing cleaveth.
Disciple:
Where is the Ground in any Soul, to which there will NoThing stick? Or, where is that which abideth and dwelleth not in SomeThing?
Master:
It is the Center of Rest and Motion in the resigned Will of a truly contrite Spirit, which is crucified to the World. This Center of the Will is impenetrable consequently to the World, the Devil, and Hell; Nothing in all the World can enter into it, or adhere to it, though never so many Devils should be in the Confederacy against it; because the Will is dead with Christ unto this World, but quickened with Him in the Center thereof, after His Blessed Image. Here it is where Man dwelleth not; and where no SELF abideth, or can abide.
Disciple:
O where is this naked Ground of the Soul void of all SELF? And how shall I come at the hidden Center where God dwelleth, and not Man? Tell me plainly, loving Sir, where it is, and how it is to be found by me, and entered into?
Master:
There where the Soul hath slain its OWN Will, and willeth no more any Thing as from itSELF, but only as God willeth, and

as His Spirit moveth upon the Soul, shall this appear. Where the Love of SELF is banished, there dwelleth the Love of God. For so much of the Soul's OWN Will as is dead unto itSELF, even so much Room hath the Will of God, which is His Love, taken up in that Soul. The Reason whereof is this; Where its OWN Will did before sit, there is now Nothing; and where Nothing is, there alone is it that the Love of God worketh.

Disciple:
But how shall I comprehend It?

Master:
If thou goest about to comprehend It, then It will fly away from thee; but if thou dost surrender thyself wholly up to It, then It will abide with thee, and become the Life of thy Life, and be natural to thee.

Disciple:
And how can this be without dying, or the whole Destruction of my Will?

Master:
Upon this entire Surrender and Yielding up of thy Will, the Love of God IN THEE becometh the Life of thy Nature; It killeth thee not, but quickeneth thee, who art now dead to thySELF in thine own Will, according to Its proper Life, even the Life of God. And then thou livest, yet not to thy own Will; but thou livest to Its Will, forasmuch as thy Will is henceforth become Its Will. So then it is no longer thy Will, but the Will of God; no longer the Love of thySELF, but the Love of God, which moveth and operateth in thee; and then, being thus comprehended in It, thou art dead indeed as to thySELF, but art alive unto God. So being dead thou livest, or rather God liveth IN THEE by His Spirit; and His Love is made to thee Life from the Dead. Never couldst thou with all thy seeking, have apprehended It; but It hath apprehended thee. Much less couldst thou have comprehended It. But now It hath comprehended thee; and so the Treasure of Treasures is found.

Disciple:

How is it that so few Souls do find It, when yet all would be glad enough to have It?

Master:

They all seek It in Somewhat, and so they find It not. For where there is Somewhat for the Soul to adhere to, there the Soul findeth but that Somewhat only, and taketh up its Rest therein, until she seeth that It is to be found in Nothing, and goeth again out of the Somewhat into Nothing, even into that Nothing out of which all Things may be made. The Soul here saith, " I have Nothing, for I am utterly empty and stripped of every Thing; I can do Nothing, for I have no Manner of Power, but am as Water poured out; I am Nothing, for all that I am is no more than an Image of Being, and only God is to me I AM; and so sitting down in my own Nothingness, I give Glory to the Eternal Being, and will Nothing of mySELF, that so God may will All in me, being unto me my God and All Things." Herein now that it is that so very few find this most precious Treasure in the Soul, though every one would so fain have It; and might also have It were it not for this or that Somewhat into which every one letteth.

Disciple:

But if the Love should proffer Itself to a Soul, could not that Soul find It, nor lay hold on It, without going for It into Nothing?

Master:

No verily. Men seek and find not, because they seek It not in the naked Ground where It lieth; but in SomeThing or Other where It never will be, neither can be. They seek It in their OWN Will, and they find It not. They seek It in their Self-Desire, and they meet not with It. They look for It in an Image, or in an Opinion, or in an Affection, or a natural Devotion and Fervour, and they lose the Substance by thus hunting after a Shadow. They search for It in Something sensible or imaginary, in Somewhat which they may have a more peculiar natural Inclination for, and Adhesion to; and so they miss of what they seek, for Want of diving into the Supersensual and Supernatural Ground where the Treasure is hid. Now should the Love graciously condescend to proffer Itself to such as these, and even to present Itself evidently before the Eye of their Spirit, yet would It find no Place in them at all, neither could It be held by them, or remain with them.

Disciple:

Why not, if the Love should be willing and ready to offer Itself, and to stay with them?

Master:

Because the Imaginariness which is in their own Will hath set up itself in the Place thereof; and so this Imaginariness would have the Love in it; but the Love fleeth away, for it is Its Prison. The Love may offer Itself; but It cannot abide where the Self-Desire attracteth or imagineth. That Will which attracteth Nothing, and to which Nothing adhereth, is the only Will capable of receiving It, for It dwelleth only in Nothing as I said, and therefore they find It not.

Disciple:

If It dwell only in Nothing, what is now the Office of It in Nothing?

Master:

The Office of the Love here is to penetrate incessantly into Something; and if It penetrate into, and find a Place in Something which is standing still and at Rest, then Its Business is to take Possession thereof. And when It hath there taken Possession, then It rejoiceth therein with Its flaming Love-Fire, even as the Sun doth in the visible World. And then the Office of it, is without Intermission to enkindle a Fire in this Something, which shall burn it up; and then with the Flames thereof exceedingly to enflame Itself and raise the Heat of the Love-Fire by It, even seven Degrees higher.

Disciple:

O loving Master, how shall I understand this?

Master:

If It but once kindle a Fire within thee, my Son, thou shalt then certainly feel how It consumeth all that which It toucheth; thou shalt feel It in the burning up of thy SELF, and swiftly devouring all Egoity, or that which thou callest I and Me, as standing in a separate Root, and divided from the Deity, the

Fountain of thy Being. And when this Enkindling is made in thee, then the Love doth so exceedingly rejoice in thy Fire, as thou wouldst not for all the World be out of It; yea, wouldst rather suffer thyself to be killed, than to enter into thy Something again. This Fire now must grow hotter and hotter, till It shall have perfected Its Office with respect to thee, and therefore wilt not give over, till It come to the seventh Degree. Its Flame hence also will be so very great, that It will never leave thee, though It should even cost thee thy temporal Life; but It would go with thee in Its sweet loving Fire into Death; and if thou wentest also into Hell, It would break Hell in Pieces also for thy Sake. Nothing is more certain than this; for It is stronger than Death and Hell.

Disciple:

Enough, my dearest Master, I can no longer endure that any Thing should divert me from It. But how shall I find the nearest Way to It?

Master:

Where the Way is hardest, there go thou; and what the World casteth away, that take thou up. What the World doth, that do thou not; but in all Things walk thou contrary to the World. So thou comest the nearest Way to that which thou art seeking.

Disciple:

If I should in all Things walk contrary to other People, I must need be in a very unquiet and sad State; and the World would not fail to account me for a Madman.

Master:

I bid thee not, Child, to do Harm to any one, thereby to create to thyself any Misery or Unquietness. This is not what I mean by walking contrary in every Thing to the World. But because the World, as the World, loveth only Deceit and Vanity, and walketh in false and treacherous Ways; thence, if thou hast a Mind to act a clean contrary Part to the Ways thereof, without any Exception or Reserve whatsoever, walk thou only in the right Way, which is called the Way of Light, as that of the World is properly called the Way of Darkness. For the right Way, even the Path of Light, is contrary to all the Ways of the World.

But whereas thou art afraid of creating to thyself hereby Trouble and Inquietude, that indeed, will be so according to the Flesh. In the World thou must have Trouble, and thy Flesh will not fail to be unquiet, and to give thee Occasion for continual Repentance. Nevertheless in this very Anxiety of Soul, arising either from the World or the Flesh, the LOVE doth most willingly enkindle Itself, and Its cheering and conquering Fire is but made to blaze forth with greater Strength for the Destruction of that Evil.

And whereas thou dost also say, that the World will for this esteem thee mad, it is true the World will be apt enough to censure thee for a Madman in Walking contrary to it. And thou art not to be surprised if the Children thereof laugh at thee, calling thee silly Fool. For the Way to the Love of God is Folly to the World, but is Wisdom to the Children of God. Hence, whenever the World perceiveth this holy Fire of Love in God's Children, it concludeth immediately that they are turned Fools, and are beside themselves. But to the Children of God, that which is despised of the World is the greatest Treasure; yea, so great a Treasure It is, as no Life can express, no Tongue so much as name what this inflaming, all-conquering Love of God is. It is brighter than the Sun; It is sweeter than any Thing that is called sweet; It is stronger than all Strength; It is more nutrimental than Food; more cheering to the Heart than Wine, and more pleasant than all the Joy and Pleasantness of this World. Whosoever obtaineth It, is richer than any Monarch on Earth; and he who getteth It, is nobler than any Emperor can be, and more potent and absolute than all Earthly Power and Authority.

"Behold, I stand at the Door and knock: if any man HEAR My voice, and open the Door, I will come in to him, and will sup with him, and he with Me."

"He that is of God HEARETH God's Words; ye therefore HEAR them not, because ye are not of God."

"My Sheep HEAR My Voice; and I know them, and they follow Me... And a Stranger will they not follow, but will flee from him: for they know not the Voice of Strangers."

"He that has Ears to HEAR, let him HEAR."

OF
HEAVEN and HELL

by

Jacob Boehme 1575-1624,
The Teutonic Theosopher

A
DIALOGUE
BETWEEN
A SCHOLAR AND HIS MASTER
SHOWING

Whither the blessed and the damned Souls go when they depart from their Bodies; and How Heaven and Hell are in Man; Where the Angels and Devils dwell in this World's Time; How far Heaven and Hell are asunder; and What and Whence the Angels and Human Souls are; What the Body of Man is; and Why the Soul is capable of receiving Good and Evil; Of the Destruction of the World; Of Man's Body in and after the Resurrection; Where Heaven and Hell shall be; Of the Last Judgement; and Why the Strife in the Creature must be.

Composed by a Soul that loveth all
who are Children of JESUS CHRIST, under the Cross.

Brought forth in the 1600's by a humble shoemaker; translated into English over 100 years later; suppressed and hidden away until recently in theological archives around the world... a worthy personal study not just for academics but for all those who are spiritually grounded in the WORD, who are learning to hear the Lord, and who hunger for more.

OF HEAVEN AND HELL
A DIALOGUE between JUNIUS, a SCHOLAR,
and THEOPHORUS, his MASTER

The Scholar asked his Master, saying;
Whither goeth the Soul when the Body dieth?
His master answered him;
There is no Necessity for it to go any whither.
What not! said the inquisitive Junius:
Must not the Soul leave the Body at Death, and go either to Heaven or Hell?
It needs no going forth, replied the venerable Theophorus:
Only the outward mortal Life with the Body shall separate themselves from the Soul. The Soul hath Heaven and Hell within itself before, according as it is written, "The Kingdom of God cometh not with Observation, neither shall they say, Lo here! or Lo there! For behold the Kingdom of God is within you." And which soever of the two, that is, either Heaven or Hell is manifested in it, in that the Soul standeth.
Here Junius said to his Master;
This is hard to understand. Doth it not enter into Heaven or Hell, as a Man entereth into a House; or as one goeth through a Hole or Casement, into an unknown Place; so goeth it not into another World?
The Master spoke and said;
No. There is verily no such Kind of entering in; forasmuch as Heaven and Hell are everywhere, being universally co-extended.
How is that possible? said the Scholar.
What, can Heaven and Hell be here present, where we are now sitting? And if one of them might, can you make me believe that both should ever be here together?
Then spoke the Master in this Manner:
I have said that Heaven is everywhere present; and it is true. For God is in Heaven; and God is everywhere. I have said also, that Hell must be in like Manner everywhere; and that is also true. For the wicked One, who is the Devil, is in Hell; and the whole

World, as the Apostle hath taught us, lieth in the wicked One, or the evil One; which is as much as to say, not only that the Devil is in the World, but also that the World is in the Devil; and if in the Devil, then in Hell too, because he is there. So Hell therefore is everywhere, as well as Heaven; which is the Thing that was to be proved.

The Scholar, startled hereat, said,

Pray make me to understand this.

To whom the Master said:

Understand then what Heaven is: It is but the Turning in of the Will into the Love of God. Wheresoever thou findest God manifesting Himself in Love, there thou findest Heaven, without travelling for it so much as one Foot. And by this understand also what Hell is, and where it is. I say unto thee, it is but the Turning in of the Will into the Wrath of God. Wheresoever the Anger of God doth more or less manifest itself, there certainly is more or less of Hell, in whatsoever Place it be. So that it is but the Turning in of thy Will either into His Love, or into His Anger; and thou art accordingly either in Heaven or in Hell. Mark it well. And this now cometh to pass in this present Life, whereof St.Paul speaking, saith, "Our Conversation is in Heaven." And the Lord Christ saith also; " My Sheep HEAR my Voice, and I know them, and they follow me, and I give them the Eternal Life; and none shall pluck them out of my Hand." Observe, he saith not, I will give them - after this Life is ended; but I give them, that is, now - in the Time of this Life. And what else is this Gift of Christ to His Followers but an Eternity of Life; which for certain, can be nowhere but in Heaven. And also if Christ be certainly in Heaven, and they who follow Him in the Regeneration are in His Hand, then are they where He is, and so cannot be out of Heaven: Yea, moreover none shall be able to pluck them out of Heaven, because it is He who holdeth them there, and they are in His Hand which nothing can resist. All therefore doth consist in the Turning in, or Entering of the Will into Heaven, by HEARING the Voice of Christ, and both Knowing Him and Following Him. And so on the contrary it is also. Understandest thou this?

His Scholar said to him;

I think, in part, I do. But how cometh this entering of the Will into Heaven to pass?

The Master answered him;

This then I will endeavour to satisfy thee in; but thou must be very attentive to what I shall say unto thee. Know then, my Son, that when the Ground of the Will yieldeth itself up to God, then it sinketh out of its own SELF, and out of and beyond all Ground and Place that is or can be imagined, into a certain unknown Deep, where God only is manifest, and where He only worketh and willeth. And then it becometh nothing to itSELF, as to its OWN Working and Willing; and so God worketh and willeth in it. And God dwells in this resigned Will; by which the soul is sanctified, and so fitted to come into Divine Rest. Now in this Case when the Body breaketh, the Soul is thoroughly penetrated all over with the Divine Love, and so thoroughly illuminated with the Divine Light, even as a glowing hot Iron is by the Fire, by which being penetrated throughout, it loseth its Darkness and becometh bright and shining. Now this is the Hand of Christ, where God's Love thoroughly inhabiteth the Soul, and is in it a shining Light, and a new glorious Life. And then the Soul is in Heaven, and is a Temple of the Holy Ghost, and is itself the very Heaven of God, wherein He dwelleth. Lo, this is the entering of the Will into Heaven and how it cometh to pass.

Be pleased, Sir, to proceed, said the Scholar,

and let me know how it fareth on the other Side.

The Master said:

The godly Soul, you see, is in the Hand of Christ, that is in Heaven, as He Himself hath told us; and in what Manner this cometh to be so, you have also heard. But the ungodly Soul is not willing in this Lifetime to come into the Divine Resignation of its Will, or to enter into the Will of God; but goeth on still in its OWN Lust and Desire, in Vanity and Falsehood, and so entereth into the Will of the Devil. It receiveth thereupon into itSELF nothing but Wickedness; nothing but Lying, Pride, Covetousness, Envy, and Wrath; and thereinto it giveth up its Will and whole

Desire. This is the Vanity of the Will; and this same Vanity or vain Shadow must also in like Manner be manifested in the Soul, which hath yielded up itself to be its Servant; and must work therein, even as the Love of God worketh in the regenerated Will, and penetrates it all over, as Fire doth Iron.

And it is not possible for this Soul to come into the Rest of God; because God's Anger is manifested in it, and worketh in it. Now when the Body is parted from this Soul, then beginneth the Eternal Melancholy and Despair; because it now findeth that it is become altogether Vanity, even a Vanity most vexatious to itself, and a distracting Fury, and a self-tormenting Abomination. Now it perceiveth itself disappointed of every Thing which it had before fancied, and blind, and naked, and wounded, and hungry, and thirsty; without the least Prospect of being ever relieved, or Obtaining so much as one Drop of Water of Eternal Life. And it feeleth itself to be a mere Devil to itself, and to be its own Vile Executioner and Tormentor; and is affrighted at its own ugly dark Form, appearing as a most hideous and monstrous Worm, and fain would flee from itself, if it could, but it cannot, being fast bound with the Chains of the Dark Nature, whereinto it had sunk itself when in the Flesh. And so not having learned nor accustomed itself to sink down into the Divine Grace, and being also strongly possessed with the Idea of God, as an Angry and Jealous God, the poor Soul is both afraid and ashamed to bring its Will into God, by which Deliverance might possibly come to it.

The Soul is afraid to do it, as Fearing to be consumed by so doing, under the Apprehension of the Deity as a mere devouring Fire. The Soul is also ashamed to do it, as being confounded at its own Nakedness and Monstrosity; and therefore would, if it were possible, hide itself from the Majesty of God, and cover its abominable Form from His most holy Eye, though by casting itself still deeper into the Darkness, wherefore then it will not enter into God; nay, it cannot enter with its false Will; yea, though it should strive to enter, yet it cannot enter into the Love, because of the Will which hath reigned in it. For such a Soul is thereby captivated in the Wrath; yea, is itself but mere Wrath, having by its false Desire, which it had awakened in itself, comprehended and shut up itself therewith, and so transformed itself into the Nature and Property thereof.

And since also the Light of God doth not shine in it, nor the Love of God incline it, the Soul is moreover a great Darkness, and is withal an anxious Fire-Source, carrying about a Hell within itself, and not being able to discern the least Glimpse of the Light of God, or to feel the least Spark of His love. Thus it dwelleth in itself as in Hell, and needeth no entering into Hell at all, or being carried thither; for in what Place soever it may be, so long as it is in itSELF, it is in the Hell. And though it should travel far, and cast itself many hundred thousand Leagues from its present Place, to be out of Hell; yet still would it remain in the Hellish Source and Darkness.

If this be so, how then cometh it, said the Scholar to Theophorus,

that a Heavenly Soul doth not in the Time of this Life perfectly perceive the Heavenly Light and Joy; and the Soul which is without God in the World, doth not also here feel Hell, as well as hereafter? Why should they not both be perceived and felt as well in this Life as in the next, seeing that both of them are in Man, and one of them (as you have shown) worketh in every Man?

To whom Theophorus presently returneth this Answer:

The Kingdom of Heaven is in the Saints operative and manifestative of itself by Faith. They who carry God within them, and live by His Spirit, find the Kingdom of God in their Faith; and they feel the Love of God in their Faith, by which the Will hath given up itSELF into God, and is made Godlike. In a Word, all is transacted within them by Faith, which is to them the Evidence of the Eternal Invisibles, and a great Manifestation in their Spirit of this Divine Kingdom, which is within them. But their natural Life is nevertheless encompassed with Flesh and Blood; and this Standing in a Contrariety thereto, and being placed through the Fall in the Principle of God's Anger, and surrounded about with the World, which by no Means can be reconciled to Faith, these faithful Souls cannot but be very much exposed to Attacks from this World, wherein they are Sojourners; neither can they be insensible of their being thus compassed about with Flesh and Blood, and with this World's vain Lust, which ceaseth not continually to penetrate the outward mortal Life, and to tempt them in manifold Ways, even as it did Christ. Whence the World on one side, and Devil on the other, not without the Curse of God's Anger in Flesh and Blood, do thoroughly penetrate and sift the Life; whereby it cometh to pass that the Soul is often in Anxiety when these three are all set upon it together, and when Hell thus assaulteth the Life, and would manifest itself in the Soul. But the Soul hereupon sinketh down into the Hope of the Grace of God, and standeth like a beautiful Rose in the Midst of Thorns, until the Kingdom of this World shall fall from it in the Death of the Body; And then the Soul first becometh truly manifest in the Love of God, and in His Kingdom, which is the Kingdom of Love; having henceforth nothing more to hinder it. But during this Life she must walk with Christ in this World; and then Christ delivereth her out of her own Hell, by penetrating her with His Love throughout, and standing by her in Hell, and even changing her Hell into Heaven.

But in that thou moreover sayest, why do not the Souls which are without God feel Hell in this World? I answer; They bear it about with them in their wicked Consciences, but they know it not; because the World hath put out their Eyes, and its deadly Cup hath cast them likewise into a Sleep, a most fatal Sleep. Notwithstanding which it must be owned that the Wicked do frequently feel Hell within them during the Time of this mortal Life, though they may not apprehend that it is Hell, because of the earthly Vanity which cleaveth unto them from without, and the sensible Pleasures and Amusements wherewith they are intoxicated. And moreover it is to be noted, that the outward Life in every such one hath yet the Light of the outward Nature, which ruleth in that Life; and so the Pain of Hell cannot, so long as that hath Rule, be revealed.

But when the Body dieth or breaketh away, so as the Soul cannot any longer enjoy such temporal Pleasure and Delight, nor the Light of this outward World, which is wholly thereupon extinguished as to it; then the Soul stands in a eternal Hunger and Thirst after such Vanities as it was here in Love withal, but yet can reach nothing but that false Will, which it had impressed in itself while in the Body; and wherein it had abounded to its great Loss. And now whereas it had too much of its Will in this Life, and yet was not contented therewith, it hath after this Separation by Death, as little of it; which createth in it an everlasting Thirst after that which it can henceforth never more obtain, and causeth it to be in a perpetual anxious Lust after Vanity, according to its former Impression, and in a continual Rage of Hunger after those Sorts of Wickedness and Lewdness whereinto it was immersed, while being in the Flesh.

Fain would it do more Evil still, but that it hath not either wherein or wherewith to effect the Same, left to it; and therefore it doth perform this only in itself. All is now internally transacted, as if it were outward; and so the Ungodly Soul is tormented by those Furies which are in his own Mind, and begotten upon himself by himself. For he is verily become his own Devil and Tormentor; and that by which he sinned here, when the Shadow of this World is passed away, abideth still with him in the Impression, and is made his Prison and his Hell. But this hellish Hunger and Thirst cannot be fully manifested in the Soul, till the Body which ministered to the Soul what it lusted after, and with which the Soul was so bewitched, as to dote thereupon, and pursue all its Cravings, be stripped off from it.

I perceive then, said Junius to his Master,

that the Soul having played the Wanton with the Body in all Voluptuousness, and having served the Lusts thereof during this Life, retaineth still the very same Inclinations and Affections which it had before; so that when it hath no more Opportunity nor Capacity to satisfy them; and when it finds it cannot, then Hell will open in that Soul, which before had been shut up, by

Means of the outward Life in the Body, and of the Light of this World. Do I rightly understand?

Theophorus said,

It is very rightly understood by you. Go on.

On the other hand, the Scholar went on,

I clearly perceive by what I have heard, that Heaven cannot but be in a loving Soul, which is possessed of God, and hath subdued thereby the Body to the Obedience of the Spirit in all Things, and perfectly immersed itself into the Will and Love of God. And when the Body dieth, and this Soul is hence redeemed from the Earth, it is now evident to me, that the Life of God which was hidden in it, will display Itself gloriously, and Heaven will consequently be then manifested. But notwithstanding, if there be not also a local Heaven besides, and a local Hell, I am still at a loss where to place no small Part of the Creation, if not the greatest. For where must all the intellectual Inhabitants abide?

In their own Principle, answered the Master, whether it be of Light or of Darkness. For every created intellectual Being remaineth in its Deeds and Essences, in its Wonders and Properties, in its Life and Image; and therein it beholdeth and feeleth God, as Who is everywhere, whether it be in the Love, or in the Wrath.

If it be in the Love of God, then beholdeth it God accordingly, and feeleth Him as He is Love. But if it hath captivated itself in the Wrath of God, then it cannot behold God otherwise than in the wrathful Nature, nor perceive Him otherwise than as an incensed and vindictive Spirit. All Places are alike to it, if it be in God's Love; and if it be not there, every Place is Hell alike. What Place can bound a Thought? Or what needeth any understanding Spirit to be kept here or there, in order to its Happiness or Misery? Verily, wheresoever it is, it is in the abyssal World, where there is neither End nor Limit. And whither, I pray, should it go? Since though it should go a thousand Miles off, or a thousand Times ten thousand Miles, and this ten thousand Times over, beyond the Bounds of the Universe, and into the imaginary Spaces above the Stars, yet it were then still in the very same Point from whence it went out. For God is the Place of Spirit; if it may be lawful to attribute to Him such a Name, to which the Body hath a Relation: And in God there is no Limit; both near and afar off is here all one; and be it in His Love, or be it in His Anger, the abyssal Will of the Spirit is altogether unconfined. It is swift as Thought, passing through all Things; it is magical, and nothing corporeal or from without can let or obstruct it; it dwelleth in its Wonders, and they are its House.

Thus it is with every Intellectual, whether of the Order of Angels, or of human Souls; and you need not fear but there will be Room enough for them all, be they ever so many; and such also as shall best suit them, even according to their Election and Determination; and which may thence very well be called his own Place.

At which, said the Scholar;

I remember, indeed, that it is written concerning the great Traitor, that he went after Death to his own Place.

The Master here said:

The same is true of every Soul, when it departeth this mortal Life: And it is true in like Manner of every Angel, or Spirit whatsoever; which is necessarily determined by its own Choice. As God is everywhere, so also the Angels are everywhere; but each one in its own Principle, and in its own Property, or (if you had rather) in its own Place. The same Essence of God, which is a Place of Spirits, is confessed to be everywhere; but the Appropriation, or Participation thereof is different to every one, according as each hath attracted magically in the Earnestness of the Will. The same Divine Essence which is with the Angels of God above, is with us also below: And the same Divine Nature which is with us, is likewise with them; but after different Manners and in different Degrees, communicated and participated.

And what I have said here of the Divine, is no less to be considered by you in the Participation of the Diabolical Essence and Nature, which is the Power of Darkness, as to the manifold

Modes, Degrees, and Appropriations thereof in the false Will. In this World there is Strife between them: but when this World hath reached in any one the Limit, then the Principle catcheth that which is its own: and so the Soul receiveth Companions accordingly, that is, either Angels or Devils.

To whom the Scholar said again:

Heaven and Hell then being in us at Strife in the Time of this Life, and God Himself being also thus near unto us, where can Angels and Devils dwell?

And the Master answered him thus:

Where thou dost not dwell as to thy SELF-hood, and to thine OWN Will, there the holy Angels dwell with thee, and everywhere all over round about thee. Remember this well. On the contrary, where thou dwellest as to thySELF, in SELF-Seeking, and SELF-Will, there to be sure the Devils will be with thee, and will take up their abode with thee, and dwell all over thee, and round about thee everywhere. Which God in his Mercy prevent.

I understand not this, said the Scholar,

so perfectly well as I could wish. Be pleased to make it a little more clear to me.

The Master then spoke:

Mark well what I am going to say. Where the Will of God in any Thing willeth, there is God manifested; and in this very manifestation of God, the Angels do dwell. But where God in any Creature willeth not with the Will of that Creature, there God is not manifested to it, neither can He be; but dwelleth in Himself, without the Co-operation and Subjection of the Creature to Him in Humility. There God is an unmanifested God to the Creature. So the Angels dwell not with such a one; for wherever they dwell, there is the Glory of God; and they make His Glory. What then dwelleth in such a Creature as this? God dwelleth not therein; the Angels dwell not therein; God willeth not therein, the Angels also will not therein. The case is evidently this, in that Soul or Creature its OWN Will is without God's Will, and there the

Devil dwelleth; and with him all whatever is without God, and without Christ. This is the Truth; lay it to Heart.

The Scholar:

It is possible I may ask several impertinent Questions; but I beseech you, good Sir, to have Patience with me, and to pity my Ignorance, if I ask what may appear to you perhaps ridiculous, or may not seem fit for me to expect an Answer to. For I have several Questions still to propound to you; but I am ashamed of my own Thoughts in this Matter.

The Master:

Be plain with me, and propose whatever is upon your Mind; yea, be not ashamed even to appear ridiculous, so that by Querying you may but become wiser.

The Scholar thanked his Master for this Liberty, and said:

How far then are Heaven and Hell asunder?

To whom he answered thus:

As far as Day and Night; or as far as Something and Nothing. They are in one another, and yet they are at the greatest Distance one from the other. Nay, the one of them is as nothing to the other; and yet notwithstanding they cause Joy and Grief to one another. Heaven is throughout the whole World, and It is also without the World over all, even everywhere that is, or that can be but so much as imagined. It filleth all; It is within all; It is without all; It encompasseth all; without Division, without Place; working by a Divine Manifestation, and flowing forth universally, but not going in the least out of Itself. For It worketh only in Itself, and is revealed, being ONE, and undivided in ALL. It appeareth only through the Manifestation of God; and never but in Itself only: And in that Being which cometh into It, or in that wherein It is manifested, there also it is that God is manifested. Because Heaven is nothing else but a Manifestation or Revelation of the Eternal ONE, wherein ALL the Working and Willing is in quiet LOVE.

So in like Manner Hell also is through the whole World, and dwelleth and worketh but in itself, and in that wherein the Foundation of Hell is manifested, namely, in SELF-hood, and in the False Will. The visible World hath both in it; and there is no Place but what Heaven and Hell may be found or revealed in it. Now Man as to his temporal Life, is only of the visible World; and therefore during the Time of this Life, he seeth not the spiritual World. For the outward World with its Substance, is a Cover to the spiritual World, even as the Body is to the Soul. But when the outward Man dieth, then the spiritual World, as to the Soul, which hath now its Covering taken away, is manifested either in the Eternal Light with the holy Angels, or in the Eternal Darkness, with the Devils.

The Scholar further queried:

What is an Angel, or a human Soul, that they can be thus manifested either in God's Love or Anger, either in Light or Darkness?

To whom Theophorus answered:

They come from one and the self-same Original: They are little Branches of the Divine Wisdom, of the Divine Will, sprung from the Divine Word, and made Objects of the Divine Love. They are out of the Ground of Eternity, whence Light and Darkness do spring: Darkness, which consisteth in the receiving of SELF-Desire: and Light, which consisteth in Willing the same Thing with God. For in the conformity of the Will with God's Will, is Heaven; and wheresoever there is this Willing with God, there the Love of God is undoubtedly in the Working, and His Light will not fail to manifest Itself. But in the SELF-Attraction of the Soul's Desire, or in the Reception of SELF into the Willing of any Spirit, Angelical or Human, the Will of God worketh difficultly, and is to that Soul or Spirit nought but Darkness; out of which, notwithstanding, the Light may be manifested. And this Darkness is the Hell of that Spirit wherein it is. For Heaven and Hell are nought else but a Manifestation of the Divine Will either in Light or Darkness, according to the Properties of the Spiritual World.

What the Body of Man is; and why the Soul is capable of receiving Good and Evil.

Scholar.

WHAT then is the Body of Man?

Master.

It is the visible World; an Image and Quintessence, or Compound of all that the World is; and the visible World is a Manifestation of the inward spiritual World, come out of the eternal Light, and out of the eternal Darkness, out of the spiritual Compaction or Connection; and it is also an Image or Figure of Eternity, whereby Eternity hath made itself visible; where SELF-Will and RESIGNED Will, viz. Evil and Good, work one with the other. Such a Substance is the outward Man. For God created Man of the outward World, and breathed into him the inward spiritual World for a Soul and intelligent Life; and therefore in the Things of the outward World, Man can receive and work Evil and Good.

Of the Destruction of the World; of Man's Body, in and after the Resurrection; where Heaven and Hell shall be; of the the Last Judgement; and wherefore the Strife in the Creature must be.

Scholar.

WHAT shall be after this World, when all Things perish and come to an End?

Master.

The material Substance only ceaseth; viz. the four Elements, the Sun, Moon, and Stars. And then the inward World will be wholly visible and manifest. But whatsoever hath been wrought by the Will or Spirit of a Man in this World's Time, whether evil or good shall not cease. I say, every such Work shall there separate itself in a spiritual Manner, either into the Eternal Light, or into the Eternal Darkness. For that which is born from each Man's Will shall penetrateth and passeth again into that which is like itself. And there the Darkness is called Hell, and is an eternal forgetting of all Good; and the Light is called the Kingdom of God, and is an eternal Joy in and to the Saints, who continually glorify and praise God, for having delivered them from the Torment of Evil.

The Last Judgement is but a Kindling of the Fire both of God's Love and Anger, in which the Matter of every Substance perisheth, and each Fire shall attract into itself its own, that is, the Substance that is like itself: Thus God's Fire of Love will draw into It whatsoever is born in the Love of God, or Love-Principle, in which also It shall burn after the Manner of Love, and yield Itself into that Substance. But the Torment will draw into itself what is wrought in the Anger of God in Darkness, and consume the false Substance; and then there will remain only the painful aching Will in its own proper Nature, Image and Figure.

Scholar.

With what Matter and Form shall the human Body rise?

Master.

It is sown a natural gross and elementary Body, which in this Lifetime is like the outward Elements; yet in this gross Body there is a subtle Power and Virtue. As in the Earth also there is a subtle good Virtue, which is like the Sun, and is one and the same with the Sun; which also in the Beginning of Time did spring and proceed out of the Divine Power and Virtue, from whence all the good Virtue of the Body is likewise derived. This good Virtue of the mortal Body shall come again and live forever in a Kind of transparent crystalline material Property, in spiritual Flesh and Blood; as shall return also the good Virtue of the Earth, for the Earth likewise shall become crystalline, and the Divine Light shine in every Thing that hath a Being, Essence or Substance. And as the gross Earth shall perish and never return, so also the gross Flesh of Man shall perish and not live forever. But all Things must appear before the Judgement, and in the Judgement be separated by the Fire; yea, both the Earth, and also the Ashes of the human Body. For when God shall once move the spiritual World, every Spirit shall attract its spiritual Substance to itself. A good Spirit and Soul shall draw to itself its good Substance, and an evil one its evil Substance. But we must here understand by Substance, such a material Power and Virtue, the Essence of which is mere Virtue, like a material Tincture (such a Thing as hath all Figures, Colors, and Virtues in it, and is at the same

Time transparent), the Grossness whereof shall have perished in all Things.

Scholar.

Shall we not rise again with our visible Bodies, and live in them forever?

Master.

When the visible World perisheth, then all that hath come out of it, and hath been external, shall perish with it. There shall remain of the World only the heavenly crystalline Nature and Form, and of Man also only the spiritual Earth; for Man shall be then wholly like the spiritual World, which as yet is hidden.

Scholar.

Shall there be Husband and Wife, or Children or Kindred, in the heavenly Life, or shall one associate with another, as they do in this Life?

Master.

Why art thou so fleshly-minded? There will be neither Husband nor Wife, but all will be like the Angels of God, Viz. Masculine Virgins. There will be neither Son nor Daughter, Brother nor Sister, but all of one Stock and Kindred. For all are but One in Christ, as a Tree and its Branches are one, though distinct as Creatures; but God is All in All. Indeed, there will be spiritual Knowledge of what every one hath been, and done, but no Possessing or Enjoying, or Desire of Possessing earthly Things, or Enjoying fleshly Relations any more.

Scholar.

Shall they all have that Eternal Joy and Glorification alike?

Master.

The Scripture saith, "Such as the People is, such is their God." And in another Place, " With the holy thou art holy, and with the perverse thou art perverse." And St.Paul saith, "In the Resurrection one shall differ from another in Glory, as do the Sun, Moon, and Stars." Therefore know, that the Blessed shall indeed all enjoy the Divine Working in and upon them; but their Virtue, and Illumination or Glory, shall be very different, according as they have been endued in this Life with different

Measures and Degrees of Power and Virtue in their painful Working. For the painful Working of the Creature in this Lifetime is the opening and begetting of Divine Power, by which that Power is made movable and operative. Now those who have wrought with Christ in this Lifetime, and not in the Lust of the Flesh, shall have great Power and transcendent Glorification in and upon them. But others, who have only expected, and relied upon, an imputed Satisfaction, and in the meanwhile have served their Belly-God, and yet at last have turned, and obtained Grace; those, I say, shall not attain to so high a Degree of Power and Illumination. So that there will be as great a Difference of Degrees between them, as is between the Sun, Moon and Stars; or between the Flowers of the Field in their Varieties of Beauty, Power, and Virtue.

Scholar.

How shall the World be judged, and by Whom?

Master.

Jesus Christ, that "Word of God which became Man," shall by the Power of His Divine Stirring or Motion separate from Himself all that belongeth not to Him, and shall wholly manifest His Kingdom in the Place or Space where this World now is; for the separating Motion worketh all over the Universe, through all at once.

Scholar.

Whither shall the Devils and all the Damned be thrown, when the Place of this World is become the Kingdom of Christ, and as Such shall be glorified? Shall they be cast out of the Place of this World? Or shall Christ have, and manifest His Dominion, out of the Sphere or Place of this World?

Master.

Hell shall remain in the Place or Sphere of this World everywhere, but hidden to the Kingdom of Heaven, as the Night is hidden in and to the Day. "The Light shall shine forever in the Darkness, but the Darkness can never comprehend, or reach it." And the Light is the Kingdom of Christ; but the Darkness is Hell, wherein the Devils and the Wicked dwell; and thus they shall be suppressed by the Kingdom of Christ, and made his Footstool, viz. a Reproach.

Scholar.

How shall all People and Nations be brought to Judgement?

Master.

The Eternal Word of God, out of which every spiritual creaturely Life hath proceeded, will move Itself at that Hour, according to Love and Anger, in every Life which is come out of the Eternity, and will draw every Creature before the Judgement of Christ, to be sentenced by this Motion of the World. The Life will then be manifested in all its Works, and every Soul shall see and feel its Judgement and Sentence in itself. For the Judgement is indeed immediately manifested in and to every Soul at the Departure of the Body; and the last Judgement is but a Return of the spiritual Body, and a Separation of the World, when the Evil shall be separated from the Good, in the substance of the World and of the human Body, and every Thing enters into its eternal Receptacle. And thus it is a Manifestation of the Mystery of God in every Substance and Life.

Scholar.

How will the Sentence be pronounced?

Master.

Here consider the Words of Christ. "He will say to those on His Right-hand, Come, ye blessed of My Father, inherit the Kingdom prepared for you from the Foundation of the World. For I was hungry, and ye gave Me Meat; I was thirsty, and ye gave Me Drink; I was a Stranger, and ye took Me in; naked, and ye clothed Me. I was sick, and ye visited Me, in Prison, and ye came unto Me". Then shall they answer Him, saying, "Lord, when saw we Thee hungry, thirsty, a Stranger, naked, sick, or in Prison, and ministered thus unto Thee?" And shall the King answer and say unto them; "Inasmuch as ye have done it unto one of the least of these my Brethren, ye have done it unto Me." And unto the Wicked on His Left-hand He will say, "Depart from Me, ye Cursed, into everlasting Fire, prepared for the Devil and his Angels. For I was hungry, thirsty, a Stranger, naked, sick, and in

Prison, and ye ministered not unto Me." And they shall also answer Him and say, " When did we see Thee thus, and ministered not unto Thee?" And He will answer them, "Verily I say unto you, inasmuch as ye have not done it unto one of the least of these, ye did it not to Me." And these shall depart into everlasting Punishment, but the Righteous into Life Eternal.

Scholar.
Loving Master, pray tell me why Christ saith, "What you have done to the least of these, you have done to Me; and what you have not done to them, neither have you done it to Me." And how doth a Man in his Working, doeth it to Christ Himself?

Master.
Christ dwelleth really and essentially in the Faith of those that wholly yield up themselves to Him, and He giveth them His Flesh for Food, and His Blood for Drink; and thus He possesseth the Ground of their Faith, according to the interior or inward Man. And a True Christian is called a Branch of the Vine Christ, and a Christian, because Christ dwelleth spiritually in him; therefore whatsoever Good any shall do to such a Christian in his bodily Necessities, it is done to Christ Himself, Who dwelleth in him. For such a Christian is not his own, but is wholly resigned to Christ, and become His peculiar Possession, and consequently the good Deed is done to Christ Himself.

Therefore also, whosoever shall withhold their Help from such a needy Christian, and forbear to serve him in his Necessity, they thrust Christ away from themselves, and despise Him in His Members. When a poor Person that belongeth thus to Christ, asketh any Thing of thee, and thou deniest it him in his Necessity, thou deniest it to Christ Himself. And whatsoever hurt any shall do to such a Christian, they do it to Christ Himself. When any mock, scorn, revile, reject, or thrust away such a one, they do all that to Christ; but he that receiveth him, giveth him Meat and Drink, or Apparel, and assisteth him in his necessities, doth it likewise to Christ, and to a Fellow-Member of his own Body.

Nay he even doth it to himself, if he be a True Christian; for we are all One in Christ, as a Tree and its Branches are.

Scholar.

How then will those subsist in the Day of that fierce Judgement, who afflict and vex the poor and distressed, and deprive them of their very Sweat; necessitating and constraining them by Force to submit to their Wills, and trampling upon them as their Footstools, only that they themselves may live in Pomp and Power, and spend the Fruits of this poor People's Sweat and Labor in Voluptuousness, Pride, and Vanity?

Master.

Christ suffereth in the Persecution of His Members. Therefore all the Wrong that such hard Exactors do to the poor Wretches under their Control, is done to Christ Himself; and falleth under His severe Sentence and Judgement! And besides that, they help the Devil to augment his Kingdom; for by such Oppression of the Poor they draw them off from Christ, and make them seek unlawful Ways to fill their Bellies. Nay, they work for, and with the Devil himself, doing the very same Thing which he doth; who, without Intermission, opposeth the Kingdom of Christ, which consisteth only in Love. All these Oppressors, if they do not turn with their whole Hearts to Christ, and minister to, or serve Him, must go into Hell-Fire, which is fed and kept alive by nothing else but such mere SELF, as that which they have exercised over the Poor here.

Scholar.

But how will it fare with those, and how will they be able to stand that severe Trial, who in this Time do so fiercely contend about the Kingdom of Christ, and slander, revile, and persecute one another for their Religion, as they do?

Master.

All such have not yet known Christ; and they are but as a Type or Figure of Heaven and Hell, striving with each other for the Victory.

All rising, swelling Pride, which contendeth about Opinions, is an Image of SELF. And whosoever hath not Faith and Humility, nor liveth in the Spirit of Christ, which is Love, is only armed with the Anger of God, and helpeth forward the Victory of the imaginary SELF, that is, the Kingdom of Darkness, and the Anger of God. For at the Day of Judgement all SELF shall be given to the Darkness, as shall also all the unprofitable Contentions of Men; in which they seek not after Love, but merely after their imaginary SELF, that they may exalt themselves by exalting and establishing their OWN Opinions; even stirring up Princes to Wars for the Sake of the same, and by that Means occasioning the Desolation of whole Countries of People. All such Things belong to the Judgement, which will separate the False from the True; and then all Images or Opinions shall cease, and all the Children of God shall dwell forever in the Love of Christ, and That in them.

All whosoever in this Time of Strife, namely, from the Fall to the Resurrection, are not zealous in the Spirit of Christ, and desirous to promote Peace and Love, but seek and strive for themSELVES only, are of the Devil, and belong to the Pit of Darkness, and must consequently be separated from Christ. For in Heaven all serve God their Creator in Humble Love.

Scholar.

Wherefore then doth God suffer such Strife and Contention to be in this Time?

Master.

The Life itself standeth in Strife, that it may be made manifest, sensible, and palpable, and that the Wisdom may be made separable and known.

The Strife also constituteth the eternal Joy of the Victory. For there will arise great Praise and Thanksgiving in the Saints from the experimental Sense and Knowledge that Christ in them hath overcome Darkness, and all the SELF of Nature, and that they are at length totally delivered from the Strife; at which they shall rejoice eternally, when they shall know how the Wicked are recompensed. And therefore God suffereth all Souls to stand in the Free-Will, that the eternal Dominion both of Love and Anger, of Light and Darkness, may be made manifest and known; and that every Life might cause and find its own Sentence in itself. For that which is now a Strife and Pain to the Saints in their wretched Warfare here, shall in the End be turned into great Joy to them; and that which hath been a Joy and Pleasure to ungodly Persons in this World, shall afterwards be turned into eternal Torment and Shame to them. Therefore the Joy of the Saints must arise to them out of Death, as the Light ariseth out of a Candle by the Destruction and Consumption of it in its Fire; that so the Life may be freed from the Painfulness of Nature, and possess another World.

And as the Light hath quite another Property than the Fire hath, for It giveth and yieldeth Itself forth; whereas the Fire draweth in and consumeth itself; so the holy Life of Meekness springeth forth through the Death of SELF-Will, and then God's Will of Love only ruleth, and doth ALL in ALL. For thus the Eternal ONE hath attained Feeling and Separability, and brought Itself forth again with the Feeling, through Death in great Joyfulness; that there might be an Eternal Delight in the Infinite Unity, and an Eternal Cause of Joy; and therefore that which was before Painfulness, must now be the Ground and cause of this Motion or stirring to the Manifestation of all Things. And herein lieth the Mystery of the hidden Wisdom of God.

Every one that asketh receiveth, every one that seeketh findeth; and to every one that knocketh it shall be opened. The Grace of our Lord Jesus Christ, and the Love of God, and the Communion of the Holy Ghost, be with us all. Amen.

THE WAY FROM DARKNESS TO TRUE ILLUMINATION

by Jacob Boehme 1575-1624,
The Teutonic Theosopher

A
DISCOURSE
BETWEEN
A SOUL HUNGRY AND THIRSTY
AFTER
THE FOUNTAIN OF LIFE, THE SWEET LOVE OF JESUS CHRIST.
AND
A SOUL ENLIGHTENED
SHOWING

Which Way one Soul should seek after and comfort another, and bring it by Means of its Knowledge into the Paths of Christ's Pilgrimage, and faithfully warn it of the thorny Way of the World, which leadeth the fallen Soul that naturally walketh therein, into the Abyss or Pit of Hell.

Composed by a Soul that loveth all
who are Children of JESUS CHRIST, under the Cross.

Brought forth in the 1600's by a humble shoemaker; translated into English over 100 years later; suppressed and hidden away until recently in theological archives around the world... a worthy personal study not just for academics but for all those who are spiritually grounded in the WORD, who are learning to hear the Lord, and who hunger for more.

THE WAY FROM DARKNESS
TO TRUE ILLUMINATION

There was a poor Soul that had wandered out of Paradise and come into the Kingdom of this World; where the Devil met with it, and said to it, "Whither dost thou go, thou Soul that art half blind?"

The Soul said,

I would see and speculate into the Creatures of the World, which the Creator hath made.

The Devil said,

How wilt thou see and speculate into them, when thou canst not know their Essence and Property? Thou wilt look upon their Outside only, as upon a graven Image, and canst not know them throughly.

The Soul said,

How may I come to know their Essence and Property?

The Devil said,

Thine Eyes would be opened to see them throughly, if thou didst but eat of that from whence the Creatures themselves are come to be good and evil. Thou wouldst then be as God Himself is, and know what the Creature is.

The Soul said,

I am now a noble and holy Creature; but if I should do so, the Creator hath said, that I should die.

The Devil said,

No, thou shouldst not die at all; but thy eyes would be opened, and thou shouldst be as God Himself is, and be Master of Good and Evil. Also, thou shouldst be mighty, powerful, and very great, as I am; all the Subtlety that is in the Creatures would be made known to thee.

The Soul said,

If I had the Knowledge of Nature and of the Creatures, I would then rule the whole World as I pleased.

The Devil said,

The whole Ground of that Knowledge lieth in thee. Do but turn thy Will and Desire from God or Goodness into Nature and the Creatures, and then there will arise in thee a Lust to taste; and so thou mayest eat of the Tree of Knowledge of Good and Evil, and by that means come to know all Things.

The Soul said,

Well then, I will eat of the Tree of Knowledge of Good and Evil, that I may rule all Things by my own Power; and be of myself a Lord on Earth, and do what I will, as God Himself doeth.

The Devil said,

I am the Prince of this World; and if thou wouldst rule on Earth, thou must turn thy Lust towards my Image, or desire to be like me, that thou mayest get the Cunning, Wit, Reason, and Subtlety, that my Image hath.

Thus did the Devil present to the Soul the Vulcan in the Mercury (the Power that is in the fiery Root of the Creature), that is the fiery Wheel of Essence or Substance, in the Form of a Serpent. Upon which,

The Soul said,

Behold, this is the Power which can do all Things. -- What must I do to get it?

The Devil said,

Thou thyself art also such a fiery Mercury. If thou dost break thy Will off from God, and bring it into this Power and Skill, then thy hidden Ground will be manifested in thee, and thou mayest work in the same Manner. But thou must eat of that Fruit, wherein each of the four Elements in itself ruleth over the other, and is in Strife; the Heat striving against the Cold, and the Cold against the Heat; and so all the Properties of Nature work feelingly. And then thou wilt instantly be as the fiery Wheel is, and so bring all Things into thine own Power, and possess them as thine own.

The Soul did so, and what happened thereupon.

Now when the Soul broke its Will thus off from God, and brought it into the Mercury, or the fiery Will (which is the Root of Life and Power), there presently arose in it a Lust to eat of the Tree of Knowledge of Good and Evil; and the Soul did eat thereof. Which as soon as it had done so, Vulcan (or the artificer in the fire) instantly kindled the fiery Wheel of its substance, and thereupon all the Properties of Nature awoke in the Soul and each began to exercise its own Lust and Desire.

First arose the Lust of Pride; a Desire to be great, mighty and powerful; to bring all Things under Subjection to it, and so to be Lord itself without Control; despising all Humility and Equality, as esteeming itself the only prudent, witty and cunning One, and accounting every Thing Folly that is not according to its own Humor and Liking.

Secondly arose the Lust of Covetousness; a Desire of Getting, which would draw all Things to itself, into its own Possession. For when the Lust of Pride had turned away the Will from God, then the Life of the Soul would not trust God any further, but would now begin to take Care for itself; and therefore brought its Desire into the Creatures, viz. into the Earth, Metals, Trees, and other Creatures. Thus the kindled fiery Life became hungry and covetous, when it had broken itself off from the Unity, Love and Meekness of God, and attracted to itself the four Elements and their Essence, and brought itself into the Condition of the Beasts; and so the Life became dark, empty and wrathful; and the heavenly Virtues and Colors went out, like a Candle extinguished.

Thirdly, there awoke in this fiery Life the stinging thorny Lust of Envy; a hellish Poison, a Property which all Devils have, and a Torment which makes the Life a mere Enmity to God, and to all Creatures. Which Envy raged furiously in the Desire of Covetousness, as a venomous Sting doth in the Body. Envy cannot endure, but hateth and would hurt or destroy that which Covetousness cannot draw to itself, by which hellish Passion the noble Love of the Soul is smothered.

Fourthly, there awoke in this fiery Life a Torment like Fire, viz. Anger; which would murder and remove out of the Way all who would not be subject to Pride. Thus the Ground and Foundation of Hell, which is called the Anger of God, was wholly manifested in this Soul. Whereby it lost the fair Paradise of God and the Kingdom of Heaven, and became such a Worm as the fiery Serpent was, which the Devil had presented to it in his own Image and Likeness. And so the Soul began to rule on Earth in a bestial Manner, and did all Things according to the Will of the Devil; living in mere Pride, Covetousness, Envy, and Anger, having no longer any true Love towards God. But there arose in the Stead thereof an evil bestial Love of filthy Lechery, Wantonness, and Vanity, and there was no Purity left in the Heart; for the Soul had forsaken Paradise, and taken the Earth into its Possession. Its Mind was wholly bent upon cunning Knowledge, Subtlety, and getting together a Multitude of earthly Things. No Righteousness nor Virtue remained in it at all; but whatsoever Evil and Wrong it committed, it covered all cunningly and subtly under the Cloak of its Power and Authority by Law, and called it by the Name of Right and Justice, and accounted it good.

The Devil came to the Soul.

Upon this the Devil drew near to the Soul, and brought it on from one Vice to another; for he had taken it captive in his Essence, and set Joy and Pleasure before it therein, saying thus to it: Behold, now thou art powerful, mighty and noble; endeavour to be greater, richer, and more powerful still. Display thy Knowledge, Wit, and Subtlety, that every one may fear thee, and stand in Awe of thee, and that thou mayest be respected, and get a great Name in the World.

The Soul did so.

The Soul did as the Devil counselled it, and yet knew not that its Counsellor was the Devil; but thought it was guided by its own Knowledge, Wit, and Understanding, and that it was doing very well and right all the While.

Jesus Christ met with the Soul.

The Soul going on in this Course of Life, our dear and loving Lord Jesus Christ, Who was come into this World with the Love and Wrath of God, to destroy the Works of the Devil, and to execute Judgement upon all ungodly Deeds, on a Time met with it, and spoke by a strong Power, viz. by His Passion and Death, into it and destroyed the Works of the Devil in it, and discovered to it the Way to His Grace, and shone upon it with His Mercy, calling it to return and repent; and promising that He would then deliver it from that monstrous deformed Shape or Image which it had gotten, and bring it into Paradise again.

How Christ wrought in the Soul

Now when the Spark of the Love of God, or the Divine Light, was accordingly manifested in the Soul, it presently saw itself with its Will and Works to be in Hell, in the Wrath of God, and found that it was a misshapen ugly Monster in the Divine Presence and the Kingdom of Heaven; at which it was so afraid, that it fell into the greatest Anguish possible, for the Judgement of God was manifested in it.

What Christ said.

Upon this the Lord Christ spoke into it with the Voice of His Grace, and said, "Repent and forsake Vanity, and thou shalt attain My Grace."

What the Soul said.

Then the Soul in its ugly misshapen Image, with the defiled Coat of Vanity, went before God, and entreated for Grace and the Pardon of its Sins, and came to be strongly persuaded in itself, that the Satisfaction and Atonement of our Lord Jesus Christ did belong to it. But the evil Properties of the Serpent, formed in the astral Spirit or Reason of the outward Man, would not suffer the Will of the Soul to come before God, but brought their Lusts and Inclinations thereinto. For those evil Properties would not die to their own Lusts, nor leave the World, for they were come out of the World, and therefore they feared the Reproach of it, in case they should have to forsake their worldly Honor and Glory.

But the poor Soul turned its Countenance towards God, and desired Grace from Him, even that He should bestow His Love upon it.

The Devil came to it again.

But when the Devil saw that the Soul thus prayed to God, and would enter into Repentance, he drew near to it, and thrust the Inclinations of the earthly Properties into its Prayers, and disturbed its good Thoughts and Desires which pressed forward towards God, and drew its thoughts back again to earthly Things that they might have no Access to Him.

The Soul sighed.

The central Will of the Soul indeed sighed after God, but the Thoughts arising in the Mind, that it should penetrate into Him, were distracted, scattered, and destroyed, so that they could not reach the Power of God. At which the poor Soul was still more afraid, and began to pray more earnestly. But the Devil with his Desire took hold of the Mercurial kindled fiery Wheel of Life, and awakened the evil Properties, so that evil or false Inclinations arose in the Soul, and went into that Thing wherein they had taken most Pleasure and Delight before.

The poor Soul would very fain go forward to God with its Will, and therefore used all its Endeavours; but its Thoughts continually fled away from God into earthly Things, and could not go to Him.

Upon this the Soul sighed and bewailed itself to God; but it seemed as if it were quite forsaken by Him, and cast out from His Presence. It could not get so much as one Look of Grace, but was in mere Anguish, Fear and Terror, and dreaded every Moment that the Wrath and severe Judgement of God would be manifested in it, and that the Devil would take hold of it and have it. And thereupon the Soul fell into such great Heaviness and Sorrow, that it became weary of all the temporal Things, which before had been its chief Joy and Happiness.

The earthly natural Will indeed desired those Things still, but the Soul would willingly leave them altogether, and desired to die to all temporal Lust and Joy whatsoever, and longed only after its first Native Country, from whence it originally came. But the Soul found itself to be far from thence, in great Distress and Want, and knew not what to do, yet resolved to enter into itself, and try to pray more earnestly.

The Devil's Opposition.

But the Devil opposed it, and withheld it so that it could not bring itself into any greater Fervency of Repentance.

He awakened the old earthly Lusts in its Heart, that they might still keep their evil Nature and false Right therein, and set them at Variance with the new-born Will and Desire of the Soul. For they would not die to their own Will and Light, but would still maintain their temporal Pleasures, and so kept the poor Soul captive in their evil Desires, that it could not stir, though it sighed and longed even more after the Grace of God. For whensoever it prayed, or offered to press forward towards God, then the Lusts of the Flesh swallowed up the Rays and Ejaculations that went forth from it, and brought them away from God into earthly Thoughts, that it might not partake of Divine Strength. Which caused the poor Soul to think itself forsaken of God, not knowing that He was so near it and did thus attract it.

Also the Devil got access to it, and entered into the fiery Mercury, or fiery Wheel of its Life, and mingled his Desires with the earthly Lusts of the Flesh, and tempted the poor Soul; saying to it in the earthly Thoughts, "Why dost thou pray? Dost thou think that God knoweth thee or regardeth thee: Consider but what Thoughts thou hast in His Presence; are they not altogether evil? Thou hast no Faith or Belief in God at all; how then should He hear thee? He heareth thee not, leave off; why wilt thou needlessly torment and vex thyself? Thou has Time enough to repent at Leisure. Wilt thou be mad? Do but look upon the World, I pray thee, a little; doth it not live in Jollity and Mirth? Yet it will be saved well enough for that. Hath not Christ paid the Ransom and satisfied all Men? Thou needest only persuade and comfort thyself that it is done for thee, and then thou shalt be saved. Thou canst not possibly in this World come to any Feeling of God; therefore leave off, and take care for thy Body, and look after temporal Glory. What dost thou suppose will become of thee, if thou turn to be so stupid and melancholy? Thou wilt be the Scorn of everybody, and they will laugh at thy Folly; and so thou wilt spend thy Days in mere Sorrow and Heaviness, which is pleasing neither to God nor Nature. I pray thee, look upon the Beauty of the World; for God hath created and placed thee in it, to be a Lord over all Creatures, and to rule them. Gather a Store of temporal Goods beforehand, that thou mayest not be beholden to the World, or stand in Need hereafter. And when Old Age cometh, or when thou growest near thy End, then there will be Time enough to prepare thyself for Repentance. God will save thee, and receive thee into the heavenly Mansions then. There is no need of such ado in vexing, bewailing, and stirring up thyself, as thou makest."

The Condition of the Soul.

In these and the like Thoughts the Soul was ensnared by the Devil, and brought into the Lusts of the Flesh, and earthly Desires; and so was bound as if it were with Fetters and strong Chains, so that it did not know what to do. It looked back a little into the World and the Pleasures thereof, but still felt in itself a Hunger after the Divine Grace, and would always rather enter into Repentance, and Favor with God. For the Hand of God had touched and bruised the Soul, and therefore it could nowhere find Rest; but always sighed within itself in Sorrow for the Sins it had committed, and longed to be rid of them. Yet it could not get true Repentance, or even the Knowledge of Sin, though it had a mighty Hunger and longing Desire after such penitential Sorrow.

The Soul being thus heavy and sad, and finding no Remedy or Rest, began to cast about where it might find a fit Place to perform true Repentance in, where it might be free from Business, Hinderances and Cares of the World; and also by what Means it might win the Favor of God. And at length it decided to take itself to some private solitary Place, and give up all worldly Employments and temporal Things; and hoped, that by being bountiful and pitiful to the Poor, it should obtain God's Mercy. Thus did it devise all Kinds of Ways to get Rest, and gain the Love, Favor, and Grace of God again. But all that it tried would not do; for its worldly Business still followed it in the Lusts of the Flesh, and it was ensnared in the Net of the Devil now, as well as before, and could not attain Rest. And though for a little while it was somewhat cheered with earthly Things, yet presently it fell to be as sad and heavy again, as it was before. The Truth was, it felt the awakened Wrath of God in itself, but knew not how that came to pass nor what ailed it. For many Times great Trouble and Terror fell upon it, which made it comfortless, sick, and faint with Fear; so mightily did the first bruising Ray or Influence of the stirring Grace work upon it. And yet it knew not that Christ was in the Wrath and severe Justice of God, and fought therein with Satan, that Spirit of Error, which was incorporated in the Soul and its Body; nor it understood not that the Hunger and Desire to turn and repent came from Christ Himself, by which it was drawn in this Manner; neither did it know what hindered it from Attaining to Divine Feeling. It knew not that itSELF was a Monster, and did bear the Image of the Serpent, in which the Devil had such Power and Access to it, and had confounded all its good Desires, Thoughts, and Motions, and brought them away from God and Goodness; concerning which Christ Himself had said, "The Devil snatcheth the Word out of their Hearts, lest they should believe and be saved."

An enlightened and regenerate Soul met the distressed Soul.

By the Providence of God, an enlightened and regenerate Soul met this poor afflicted and distressed Soul, and said,"What ailest thou, thou distressed Soul, that thou art so restless and troubled?"

The distressed Soul answered,

The Creator hath hid His Countenance from me, so that I cannot come to His Rest; therefore I am thus troubled, and know not what I shall do to get His Loving-kindness again. For I feel as though great Cliffs and Rocks lie in my Way to His grace, so that I cannot come to Him. Though I sigh and long after Him ever so much, yet I am kept back so that I cannot partake of His Power, Virtue and Strength.

The enlightened Soul said,

Thou bearest the monstrous Shape of the Devil, and art clothed therewith; in which, being his own Property or Principle, he hath Access or Power of Entrance into thee, and thereby keepeth thy Will from penetrating into God. For if thy Will might penetrate into God, it would be anointed with the highest Power and Strength of God, in the Resurrection of our Lord Jesus Christ; and that Unction would break in Pieces the Monster which thou carriest about within thee; and thy first Image of Paradise would revive in the Center; which would destroy the Devil's Power therein, and thou wouldst become as an Angel again. And because the Devil envieth thee this Happiness, he holdeth thee captive in his Desire in the Lusts of the Flesh; from which if thou art not delivered, thou wilt be separated from God, and canst never enter into our Society.

The distressed Soul terrified.

At this Speech the poor distressed Soul was so terrified and amazed, that it could not speak one Word more. When it found that it stood in the Form and Condition of the Serpent, which separated it from God; and that the Devil was so near to it in that Condition, who injected evil Thoughts into the Will of the Soul, and had so much Power over it thereby, that it was near Damnation, and sticking fast in the Abyss or bottomless Pit of Hell, in the Anger of God; it would have even given up any hope for the Divine Mercy; except for the Power, Virtue and Strength of the first Stirring of the Grace of God, which had before bruised the Soul, - this upheld and preserved it from total Despair. But still it wrestled in itself between Hope and Doubt; whatsoever Hope built up was thrown down again by Doubt. And thus was it agitated with such continual Disquiet, that at last the World and all the Glory thereof became loathsome to it, neither would it enjoy worldly Pleasures any more; and yet for all this, it could not come to Rest.

The enlightened Soul came again, and spoke to the troubled Soul.

On a Time the enlightened Soul came again to this Soul, and finding it still in so great Trouble, Anguish and Grief of Mind, said to it: What doest thou? Wilt thou destroy thyself in thy Anguish and Sorrow? Why dost thou torment thyself in thy OWN Power and Will, who art but a Worm, seeing thy Torment increaseth thereby more and more? Yea, if thou shouldst sink thyself down to the Bottom of the Sea, or couldst fly to the uttermost Coasts of the Morning, or raise thyself above the Stars, yet thou wouldst not be released. For the more thou grievest, tormentest, and troublest thyself, the more painful thy Nature will be; and yet thou wilt not be able to come to any Rest. For thy Power is quite lost; and as a dry Stick burnt to a Coal cannot grow green and spring afresh by its OWN Power, nor get Sap to flourish again with other Trees and Plants, so neither canst thou reach the Place of God by thy OWN Power and Strength, and transform thyself into that Angelical Image which thou hadst at first. For in respect to God thou art withered and dry, like a dead Plant that hath lost its Sap and Strength, and so art become a dry tormenting Hunger. Thy Properties are like Heat and Cold, which continually strive one against the other, and can never unite.

The distressed Soul said,

What then shall I do to bud forth again, and recover the first Life, wherein I was at Rest before I became an Image?

The enlightened Soul said,

Thou shouldst do Nothing at all but forsake thy OWN Will, viz. that which thou callest I, or thy SELF. By which Means all thy evil Properties will grow weak, faint, and ready to die; and then thou wilt sink down again into that One Thing, from which thou art originally sprung. For now thou liest captive in the Creatures; but if thy Will forsaketh them, the Creatures, with their evil Inclinations, will die in thee, which at present stay and hinder thee so that thou canst not come to God. But if thou takest this Course, thy God will meet thee with His infinite Love, which He hath manifested in Christ Jesus in the Humanity, or Human Nature. And that will impart Sap, Life, and Vigour to thee; whereby thou mayest bud, spring, and flourish again, and rejoice in the Living God, as a Branch growing on His True Vine. And so thou wilt at length recover the Image of God, and be delivered from the Image or Condition of the Serpent: Thenshalt thou come to be my Brother, and have Fellowship with the Angels.

The poor Soul said,

How can I forsake my Will, so that the Creatures which lodge therein may die, seeing I must be in the World, and also have need of it as long as I live?

The enlightened Soul said,

Now thou hast worldly Power and Riches, which thou possesses as thy OWN, to do what thou wilt with, and regardest not how thou gettest or usest the same; employing them in the Service and Indulgence of thy OWN carnal and vain Desires. Nay, though thou seest the poor and needy Wretch, who wanteth thy Help, and is thy Brother, yet thou helpest him not, but layest heavy Burdens upon him, by requiring more of him than his Abilities will bear, or his Necessities afford; and oppressest him, by forcing him to spend his Labor and Sweat for thee, and for the Gratification of thy voluptuous Will. Thou art moreover proud, and insultest over him, and behavest roughly and sternly to him, exalting thyself above him, and making small Account of him in Respect to thyself. Then that poor oppressed Brother of thine cometh, and complaineth with Sighs towards God, that he cannot reap the Benefit of his Labor and Pains, but is forced by thee to live in Misery.

By which Sighings and Groanings of his, he raiseth up the Wrath of God in thee; which maketh thy Flame and Unquietness still the greater. These are the Creatures which thou art in Love with, and hast broken thyself off from God for their Sakes, and brought thy Love into them, or them into thy Love, so that they live therein. Thou nourishest and keepest them by continually receiving them into thy Desire, for they live in and by thy receiving them into thy Mind; because thou thereby bringest the Lust of thy Life into them. They are but unclean, filthy, and evil Births, and Issues of the bestial Nature, which yet, by thy receiving them in thy Lust or Desire, have gotten an Image, and formed themselves in thee. And that Image is a Beast with four Heads; First, Pride. Secondly, Covetousness. Thirdly, Envy. Fourthly, Anger. And in these four Properties the Foundation of Hell consisteth, which thou carriest in thee and about thee. It is imprinted and engraven in thee, and thou art wholly taken

Captive thereby. For these Properties live in thy natural Life; and thereby thou art severed or cut off from God, neither canst thou ever come to Him, unless thou so forsake these evil Creatures that they may die in thee.

But since thou desirest me to tell thee how to forsake thy own perverse creaturely Will so that the Creatures in thee might die, and how yet thou mightest live along with them in the World, I must assure thee that there is but one Way to do it, which is narrow and straight, and will be very hard and irksome to thee at the Beginning, but afterwards thou wilt walk in it cheerfully.

Thou must seriously consider, that in the Course of this worldly Life thou walkest in the Anger of God and in the Foundation of Hell; and that this is not thy true Native Country; but that a True Christian should, and must live in Christ, and in his Walking truly follow Him; and that he cannot be a True Christian, unless the Spirit and Power of Christ so live in him, that he becometh wholly Subject to It. Now seeing the Kingdom of Christ is not of this World, but in Heaven, therefore thou must always be in a continual Ascension towards Heaven, if thou wilt follow Christ; though thy Body must dwell among the Creatures and use them.

The narrow Way to which perpetual Ascension into Heaven and Imitation of Christ is this: Thou must despair of all thy OWN Power and Strength, for in and by thy OWN Power thou canst not reach the Gates of God; and firmly purpose and resolve wholly to give thyself up to the Mercy of God, and to sink down with thy whole Mind and Reason into the Passion and Death of our Lord Jesus Christ, always desiring to persevere in the same, and to die from all thy Creatures therein. Also thou must resolve to watch and guard thy Mind, Thoughts and Inclinations that they admit no Evil into them, neither must thou suffer thyself to be held fast by temporal Honor or Profit. Thou must resolve likewise to put away from thee all Unrighteousness, and whatsoever else may hinder the Freedom of thy Motion and Progress. Thy Will must be wholly pure, and fixed in a firm Resolution never to return to its old Idols any more, but that thou wilt leave them the very Instant they are known to thee, and separate thy Mind from them, and enter into the sincere Way of Truth and Righteousness, according to the plain and full Doctrine of Christ. And as thou dost thus purpose to forsake the Enemies of thine own inward Nature, so also must thou forgive all thy outward Enemies, and resolve to meet them with thy Love; so that there may be left no Creature, Person, or Thing at all able to take hold of thy Will and captivate it; but that it may be sincere, and purged from all Creatures.

Nay further; if it should be required, thou must be willing and ready to forsake all thy temporal Honor and Profit for Christ's sake, and regard nothing that is Earthly so as to set thy Heart and Affections upon it; but esteem thyself in whatsoever State, Degree, and Condition thou art, as to worldly Rank or Riches, to be but a Servant of God and of thy Fellow-Christians; or as a Steward in the Office wherein thy Lord hath placed thee. All Arrogance and SELF-Exaltation must be humbled, brought low, and so annihilated that nothing of thine OWN or of any other Creature may stay in thy Will to bring thy Thoughts or Imagination to be set upon it.

Thou must also firmly impress it on thy Mind, that thou shalt certainly partake of the promised Grace in the Merit of Jesus Christ, viz. of His outflowing Love, which indeed is already in thee, and which will deliver thee from thy Creatures, and enlighten thy Will, and kindle it with the Flame of Love, whereby thou shalt have Victory over the Devil. Not as if thou couldst will or do anything in thine OWN Strength, but only enter into the Suffering and Resurrection of Jesus Christ, and take them to thyself, and with them assault and break in Pieces the Kingdom of the Devil in thee, and mortify thy Creatures. Thou must resolve to enter into this Way this very Hour, and never to depart from it, but willingly to submit thyself to God in all thy Endeavours and Doings, that He may do with thee what He pleaseth.

When thy Will is thus prepared and resolved, it hath then broken through its own Creatures, and is sincere in the Presence of God, and clothed with the merits of Jesus Christ. It may then freely go to the Father with the Prodigal Son, and fall down in His Presence and pour forth its Prayers; and putting forth all its Strength in this Divine Work, confess its Sins and Disobedience; and how far it hath departed from God. This must be done not with bare Words, but with all its Strength, which indeed amounteth only to a strong Purpose and Resolution; for the Soul of itself hath no Strength or Power to effect any good Work.

Now when thou art thus ready, and that thy Heavenly Father shall see thy coming and returning to Him in such Repentance and Humility, He will inwardly speak to thee, and say in thee, "Behold this is My Son which I had lost; he was dead and is alive again." And He will come and meet thee in thy Mind with the Grace and Love of Jesus Christ, and embrace thee with the Beams of His Love, and kiss thee with His Spirit and Strength; and then thou shalt receive Grace to pour out thy Confession before Him, and to pray powerfully. This indeed is the right Place where thou must wrestle in the Light of His Countenance. And if thou standest resolutely here, and shrinkest not back, thou shalt see or feel great Wonders. For thou shalt find Christ in thee assaulting Hell, and crushing thy Beasts in Pieces, and that a great Tumult and Misery will arise in thee; also thy secret undiscovered Sins will then first awake, and labor to separate thee from God, and to keep thee back. Thus shalt thou truly find and feel how Death and Life fight one against the other, and shalt understand by what passeth within thyself, what Heaven and Hell are. At which Time be not moved, but stand firm and shrink not; for at length all thy Creatures will grow faint, weak, and ready to die; and then thy Will shall wax stronger, and be able to subdue and keep down the evil Inclinations. So shall thy Will and Mind ascend into Heaven every day, and thy Creatures gradually die away. Thou wilt get a Mind wholly new, and begin to be a new Creature, and getting rid of the Bestial deformity, recover the Divine Image. Thus shalt thou be delivered from thy present Anguish, and return to thy Original Rest.

The poor Soul's Practice.

Then the poor Soul began to practice this Course with such Earnestness, that it conceived it should get the Victory presently; but it found that the Gates of Heaven were shut against it in its own Strength and Power and it was as if it were rejected and forsaken by God, and received not so much as one Look or Glimpse of Grace from Him. Upon which it said to itself, "Surely thou hast not sincerely submitted thyself to God. Desire Nothing at all of Him, but only submit thyself to His Judgement and Condemnation, that He may kill thy evil Inclinations. Sink down into Him beyond the Limits of Nature and Creature, and submit thyself to Him, that He may do with thee what He will, for thou art not worthy to speak to Him."

Accordingly the Soul took a Resolution to sink down, and to forsake its own Will; and when it had done so, there fell upon it presently the greatest Repentance that could be for the Sins it had committed; and it bewailed bitterly its ugly Shape, and was truly and deeply sorry that the evil Creatures did dwell within it. And because of its Sorrow it could not speak one more Word in the Presence of God, but began in its Repentance to realize the bitter Passion and Death of Jesus Christ, viz. what great Anguish and Torment He had suffered for its Sake, in order to deliver it out of its Anguish, and change it into the Image of God. In which Consideration it wholly sunk down, and did Nothing but complain of its Ignorance and Negligence, and that it had not been thankful to its Redeemer, nor once considered the great Love He had shown to it, but had idly spent its Time, and not at all regarded how it might come to partake of His purchased and proffered Grace; but instead thereof had formed in itself the Images and Figures of earthly Things, with the vain Lusts and Pleasures of the World. Whereby it had gotten such bestial Inclinations, that now it must lie captive in great Misery, and for very shame dared not lift up its Eyes to God, Who hid the Light of His Countenance from it, and would not so much as look upon it. And as it was thus sighing and crying, it was drawn into the Abyss or Pit of Horror, and laid itself as it were at the Gates of Hell, there to perish.

Upon which the poor troubled Soul was as it were bereft of Sense, and wholly forsaken, so that it in a Manner forgot all its Doings, and would willingly yield itself to Death, and cease to be a Creature. Accordingly it did yield itself to Death, and desired Nothing else but to die and perish in the Death of its Redeemer, Jesus Christ, Who had suffered such Torments and Death for its Sake. And in this Perishing it began to sigh and pray in itself very inwardly to the Divine Goodness, and to sink down into the mere Mercy of God.

Upon this there suddenly appeared unto it the amiable Countenance of the Love of God, which penetrated through it as a great Light, and made it exceedingly joyful. It then began to pray aright, and to thank the Most High for such Grace, and to rejoice abundantly, that it was delivered from the Death and Anguish of Hell. Now it tasted of the Sweetness of God, and of His promised Truth; and now all the evil Spirits which had harassed it before, and kept it back from the Grace, Love, and inward Presence of God, were forced to depart from it. The "Wedding of the Lamb" was now kept and solemnized, that is, the Noble Sophia [or the Eternal Wisdom] espoused or betrothed herself to the Soul; and the Seal-Ring of Christ's Victory was impressed into its Essence, and it was received to be a Child and Heir of God again.

When this was done, the Soul became very joyful, and began to work in this new Power, and to celebrate with Praise the Wonders of God, and thought thenceforth to walk continually in the same Light, Strength, and Joy. But it was soon assaulted; from without, by the Shame and Reproach of the World, and from within, by great Temptation, so that it began to doubt whether its Ground was truly from God, and whether it had really partaken of His Grace.

For the Accuser, Satan, went to it, and would fain lead it out of this Course, and make it doubtful whether it was the true Way; whispering thus to it inwardly: "This happy Change in thy Spirit is not from God, but only from thine own Imagination." Also the

Divine Light retired in the Soul, and shone but in the inward Ground, as Fire raked up in Embers, so that Reason was perplexed, and thought itself forsaken, and the Soul knew not what had happened to itself, nor whether it had really and truly tasted of the heavenly Gift or not.

Yet it could not leave off struggling; for the burning Fire of Love was sown in it, which had raised in it a vehement and continual Hunger and Thirst after Divine Sweetness. So at length it began to pray aright, and to humble itself in the Presence of God, and to examine and try its evil Inclinations and Thoughts and to put them away. By which means the Will of its Reason was broken, and the evil Inclinations inherent in it were killed and extirpated more and more. This Process was very severe and painful to the Nature of the Body, for it made it faint and weak, as if it had been very sick; and yet it was no natural Sickness that it had, but only the Melancholy of its earthly Nature which was feeling and lamenting the Destruction of its evil Lusts.

Now when the earthly Reason found itself thus forsaken, and the poor Soul saw that it was despised outwardly, and derided by the World, because it would no longer walk in the Way of Wickedness and Vanity; and also that it was inwardly assaulted by the Accuser, Satan, who mocked it, and continually set before it the Beauty, Riches, and Glory of the World, and called it a Fool for not embracing them; it began to think and say thus within itself; "O eternal God! What shall I now do to come to Rest?"

The enlightened Soul met it again, and spoke to it.

While it was in this Consideration, the enlightened Soul met with it again, and said, "What ailest thou, my Brother, that thou art so heavy and sad?"

The distressed Soul said,

I have followed thy Counsel, and thereby attained a Ray, or Emanation of the Divine Sweetness, but it is gone from me again. and I am now deserted. Moreover I have outwardly very great Trials and Afflictions in the World; for all my good Friends forsake and scorn me; and am also inwardly assaulted with Anguish and Doubt, and know not what to do.

The enlightened Soul said,

Now I like thee very well; for now our beloved Lord Jesus Christ is performing that same Pilgrimage or Process on Earth with thee and in thee, which He did Himself when He was in this World, Who was continually reviled, despised, and evil spoken of and had nothing of His own in it; and now thou bearest His Mark or Badge. But do not wonder at it, or think it strange; for it must be so, in order that thou mayest be tried, refined, and purified. In this Anguish and Distress thou wilt necessarily hunger and cry after Deliverance; and by such Hunger and Prayer thou wilt attract Grace to thee both from within and from without.

For thou must grow from above and from beneath to be the Image of God again. Just as a young Plant is agitated by the Wind, and must stand its Ground in Heat and Cold, drawing Strength and Virtue to it from above and from beneath by that Agitation, and must endure many a Tempest, and undergo much Danger before it can come to be a Tree, and bring forth Fruit. For through that Agitation the Virtue of the Sun moveth in the Plant, whereby its wild Properties come to be penetrated and tinctured with the Solar Virtue, and grow thereby.

And this is the Time wherein thou must play the Part of a valiant Soldier in the Spirit of Christ, and co-operate thyself Therewith. For now the Eternal Father by His fiery Power begetteth His Son in thee, who changeth the Fire of the Father, namely, the first Principle, or wrathful Property of the Soul, into the Flame of Love, so that out of Fire and Light (viz. Wrath and Love) there cometh to be ONE Essence, Being, or Substance, which is the true Temple of God. And now thou shalt bud forth out of the Vine Christ, in the Vineyard of God, and bring forth Fruit in thy Life, and by assisting and instructing others, show forth thy Love in Abundance, as a good Tree. For Paradise must thus spring up again in thee, through the Wrath of God, and Hell be changed into Heaven in thee.

Therefore be not dismayed at the Temptations of the Devil, who seeketh and striveth for the Kingdom which he once had in thee; but having now lost it, he must be confounded, and depart from thee. And he covereth thee outwardly with the Shame and Reproach of the World, that his own Shame may not be known, and that thou mayest be hidden to the World.

For with thy new Birth or regenerated Nature, thou art in the Divine Harmony in Heaven. Be patient, therefore, and wait upon the Lord; and whatsoever shall befall thee, take it all from His Hands, as intended by Him for thy highest Good. And so the enlightened Soul departed from it.

The distressed Soul's Course.

The distressed soul began its Course now under the patient Suffering of Christ, and depending solely upon the Strength and Power of God in it, entered into Hope.

Thenceforth it grew stronger every Day, and its evil Inclinations died more and more in it. So that it arrived at length to a High State or Degree of Grace; and the Gates of the Divine Revelation and the Kingdom of Heaven, were opened to, and manifested in it.

And thus the Soul through Repentance, Faith, and Prayer, returned to its Original and True Rest, and became a Right and Beloved Child of God again; to which may He of His Infinite Mercy help us all. Amen.

"But ye are a chosen Generation, a royal Priesthood, a holy Nation, a peculiar People; that ye should show forth the Praises of Him Who hath called you out of Darkness into His marvellous Light."

Made in the USA
Middletown, DE
25 July 2021